Ohiopyle

That Little Town, WWII

Lillian "Jimmy" McCahan

That Little Town was written by Ohiopyle, Pennsylvania's Western Maryland Railroad Agent, Lillian "Jimmy" McCahan, from September 1946 – September 1947. She chronicled the year in Ohiopyle when World War II soldiers returned home. During the war, McCahan kept over 100 area soldiers in contact and informed about each other through her column, "Our Soldiers." It was published in the community and church papers, The *Messenger* and *Chimes*. She mailed them to the soldiers every month for several years, all over the world.

Edited, Organized, and Designed by Marci Lynn McGuinness
Transcribed by Brynn Cunningham

ISBN # 978-0-938833-44-4
Publisher by Shore Publications, Chalk Hill, PA

Purchase copies at www.ohiopyle.info, or order autographed copies by mail for $20. per copy (includes tax and s/h) to:
Shore Publications, P. O. Box 111, Chalk Hill, PA 15421.

Cover Photo

The scene of Ohiopyle on the cover is from a post card entitled, "Bird's Eye View of Ohiopyle, PA Showing Chestnut Ridge Mts." At the time (years ago) Pat Hall Collins gave me this card, I did not realize its significance. I do remember the look on her face, though, and thank God I recently discovered why it was important to her. Dale Collin's mother mailed it to him on December 1, 1941, 6 days before Pearl Harbor. It is also postmarked December 3, 1941.

As you can see on the post card's back side (below), he moved and probably did not receive the card until after the attack that started the war. Dale was a radio operator in the Air Corp. He has been missing, along with the bomber and crew, since a flight in the South Pacific in October, 1942.

The front of the post card shows the Western Maryland Railroad Station (today's Ohiopyle Visitor Center) to the left on the "town" side of the river. The B&O tracks are in the foreground. The Western Maryland RR Bridge and Yough Bridge are also shown. The WMD RR Bridge was torn down to make way for the "Yough" Bike/Hike trail bridge which is part of the Great Allegheny Passage today.

This book is dedicated to our soldiers.

A big thanks to Ross Rogalski, who sent Lillian McCahan's original manuscripts, diaries, note pads, and letters from World War II Ohiopyle area soldiers, to Marci Lynn McGuinness. He found them while cleaning out his parents' Connellsville home on 8th Street. Lillian had formerly lived there. I appreciate his determination in seeing that this woman who did so much for Ohiopyle, can continue her mission.

This book is in memory of Ross' wife, Martha, who passed away this June after a long battle with cancer. She also left behind young twin boys, Gus and Leo. God Bless them.

Contents

Editor's Notes

In 1940, Ohiopyle's Western Maryland Railroad Agent and author, Lillian "Jimmy" McCahan, wrote a book called *A Little Town*. She had already written *Nobody Out but Railroaders* and *Railroad Reminiscence*. The prolific writer spent a year writing about Ohiopyle happenings for the book.

During World War II, she wrote for the local church and community magazines, *The Messenger* and *Chimes*. Through her column, "Our Soldiers," she kept Ohiopyle and mountain area soldiers in touch with each other by printing where they were, mailing the magazines out to the young men all over the world, and printing some of the many letters the soldiers sent to her.

Two years ago, two boxes arrived on my doorstep. The return address was from Derby, Kansas. The name was Ross Rogalski. It is with distinct honor that I became the "Messenger" of McCahan's 1946 manuscript, "That Little Town."

While sorting through the contents of the boxes, I found letters from men I had known. Monroe Daniels, Jesse Hall, Sr., Harry and Till King, Phil Gosnell, Jack Kurtz, Jim Hochstetler, and dozens more, totaling 64 men and over 100 letters.

It took time to realize the manuscripts' significance, but coupled with the soldier's letters, it became evident that this was a book that needed to be published.

I remember Lillian and her sister, Emily, who had hip problems and could not walk well. As a fellow writer, I wish I had known she wrote back then. I was writing stories by age 6. It would have been great to know someone who was like me in that fashion.

In addition to Lillian's book (written 66 years ago), *That Little Town,* I have listed the names of the WWII soldiers whose letters I possess. The second list includes the postmarked dates on the envelopes, and quotes from some of the letters.

The letters are placed in a chapter before the book. That is chronologically, the way it happened, in *That Little Town.*

Honored,
Marci Lynn McGuinness

Ohiopyle World War II Soldier Letters to McCahan

Anna Abbey
Springer "Jack" Anderson
Clyde J. Barkley
Bailey H. Bryner
Melvin Bungard
Donald Burnsworth
Wendell Burnsworth
Earl C. Burnworth
Kenneth Cole
Lewis Collins
John Cox
Arnold Monroe Daniels
Calvin Darrow
Charles Davis
Dick DeBerry
Doran M. Ellis
Herman Geska
Phill Gosnell
Frank Hall
Jesse Hall
Robert . Hall
Don Harbaugh
E.F. Hinebaugh
James Helterbran
Jim Hochstettler
Ed Holiday
Ed Jackson
James Jennings
Harry King
Till King

Jack Kurtz
Warren Leonard
Dan Livingston
Albert Lowry
Forrest Martin
Lou Martin
Richard Martin
Wayne McCartney
Morris "Sparkie" McFarland
R.S. McMahan
Elmer "Bud" Morrison
Harold Morrison
MacDonald Morrison
Willard Rafferty
Glen Ravenscraft
G.E. Schaefer
Herbert Shipley
Lloyd Shipley
Loren Show
Frederick C. Silbaugh
Oda A. Sillings, Jr.
Olaf Skinner
Nettie C. Sproul
Robert Taylor
Lewis Taylor
Hampton Teets
Thomas Thorpe
Alfred Tressler
Kenneth G. Turner
Harold Robert Whipkey
Ralph Whipkey
Bob Wildey
Jim Williams
R. Wolfe

The following list shows when each soldier wrote the letter/s to McCahan, where he was (if possible), and includes quotes from many of the men. I am also including pages from McCahan's column and soldier's letters from the *Messenger*. Richard Martin, Dick DeBerry, and Dan Livingston wrote many letters to McCahan. All their dates are not listed.

1942

Cpl. Morris "Sparkie" McFarland, Bellows Field, February 2, 1942

"After trying many times to express my appreciation for your most wonderful Christmas gift, I have decided to just say, "Thanks a lot."

Your book of verse expresses that part of our lives that was so easily forgotten, and when remembered, so humbly cherished. I had forgotten the old oak tree, the frog pond, and those people who had worried so much about our well being.

If there had not been so many mosquitoes, I could have almost thought that the white sands of Hawaii, bathed in the moonlight, was that snow-bound Christmas in Ohiopyle.

In closing I wish to thank you again and may 1942 be as happy as your past, as anybody could be no more happy than one with so gifted an outlook on life. And may Ohiopyle, as in the past, continue to be the happy-go-lucky town in the best old state in the Union.

Keep the trains moving, and we'll keep the bombers flying."
Sparkie

Killed in Action – Cpl. Morris "Sparkie" McFarland was a member of the air corps serving in Pearl Harbor when it was bombed on December 7, 1941. The Ohiopyle native was killed in action during the autumn of 1942. He was believed to be shot down during the fighting at Port Moresby, New Guinea. Morris "Sparkie" McFarland (left) was Ohiopyle's first loss in the early days of World War II. Both he and Dale Collins (cover postcard), were shot down in-flight and lost at sea in the

fall of '42. "Sparkie" is shown here with Jim Marietta in happier times. He was the brother of Donna McFarland Rose.

Cpl. Earl C. Burnworth, Camp Hood, TX, December 15, 1942. "Received your card. It sure seemed nice to get a picture of something back in good old Ohiopyle. Looks like you are having some winter back there."

Cpl. Harold Robert Whipkey, Banksdale Field, LA, December 16, 1942. "I received the nice Christmas card you sent and you don't know how much I appreciated it. I guess my mother is working all the time at the hotel (Hazel Marietta Whipkey). She sure does work hard. This is the best field I have been in. This is one of the largest air bases. I hear from home often. I sure do enjoy it."

Sgt. Harold King, Co. E. 341st Engineers, c/o Seattle WA, December 19, 1942. " I want to thank you for the Christmas greetings card you sent me. I think it was awful nice. I am glad to know that the people of Ohiopyle are still keeping faith in God. That will go a long ways in keeping them and our country safe."

Robert Taylor, S2/c, Jacksonville, FL, December 30, 1942. "I'm down here going to Aviation Mechanic Mate School. The first dog gone thing they learn you is the Morse Code. I am having an awful time learning it. All I could do down here is dream of a White Christmas. Tell Dad to tell Mom to hurry up and write. I haven't received a letter since I have been down here."

Pvt. Lloyd Whipkey, San Franciso, CA, December 30, 1942

1943

Sgt. Dan Livingston, October 8, 1943. "Well, Mac, if you can connive a way to get me out of this thing, I'll beat a teletype key for you, make love to you or stand on the corner and beat a drum for the Salvation Army. With no intent to offend, and my kindest regards."

Lt. Robert Wildey, Italy, November 1, 1943. "I have left Africa and am now somewhere in Italy. Your article about Fall in Ohiopyle was very descriptive. Brought back fond memories. I sure hope I get to see next Fall in Ohiopyle. Your column, Our Soldiers, is a source of invaluable information to a soldier separated from all his old school mates and friends."

Cpl. Clyde J. Barkley, New Orleans, LA, November 18, 1943.

R. C. Bob Taylor, November 24, 1943. "I wish this darn war was over. If I ever get back to Ohiopyle, I never will leave there again. It sure was bad news to hear Grandmother is dead. Can you send me Jim Marietta's address? I had it but lost it with other things in Jacksonville."

P.F.C Nettie C. Sproul, General Hospital, Fort Bragg, NC, December 6, 1943. "I talked to both Roy Cunningham and Randall Hall while I was at Ft. Knox. Neither of them knew me in civilian life."

Cpl. Lloyd Shipley, December 14, 1943. "You asked about over here. It may have been a beautiful place in peace time but it is not so good now. We do not have to put up with snow, but I sure wish I could make a few snow balls for old times. I wish you and all the boys in the service a Merry Christmas and a Happy New Year.

Christmas Greetings

To All Our Soldiers

Snowflakes fell silently all day,
Heaped hills and street with white, and lay
Mounded on walls and naked trees;
They settled solid in the night
With icy crust next morning's light
Transformed to diamond tapestry.

Folks crunched it, bustling to and fro
On errands through the brilliant snow,
Preparing for their Christmas;
The graying postmistress lacked time
To talk to friends who stood in line
With parcels she must not delay.

When I sought ground-pine on the hill
The leafless woods were breathless still,
As though immersed in vesper prayer;
Rooted in snow, beneath white sky,
The trees reached motionless limbs high
Into late afternoon's chill air.

I climbed the path with reverent tread,
Brushed snow aside and found the bed
Where grew the pungent evergreen;
I filled my arms high as I could
And softly left the devout wood,
Feeling by worshippers unseen.

Emerging from that chapel dim
As early dusk was closing in,
I heard one lone bird sharply call,
And found a clear sky stained with rose,
As must have looked day at its close
When Mary rested in a stall.

                —Lillian McCahan

1944

Cpl. Arnold Monroe Daniels, Africa, January 9, 1944

Cpl. Alfred Tressler, Shreveport, LA, March 4, 1944, "Before we know it we'll be back in camp where we have nice soft beds to sleep on, and cold and hot running water, instead of sleeping in a nice cozy fox hole where there is plenty of running water, but it's all cold. I wish our boys over seas all the luck in the world, and hope our dear Lord brings them home safe."

Sgt. Edward Jackson, L. A., CA, March 3, 1944, "I am chief of a gun squad and believe I have the best gun section there is. I sure was glad to hear some of the boys are getting home for a few days. And sure hope that by the Grace of God and our prayers we will all be back together soon."

When I (Marci McGuinness) read the above letter, I thought it was from another **Ed Jackson, who is 89 years old today**. This was his cousin, but I visited Ed, who lives near Ohiopyle, and remembers the day Pearl Harbor was attacked.

"I was 18 and knew where I was going when we heard it on the radio, to the service."

Ed is a young looking man, as is his wife. "I don't know why I am alive," he said, then proceeded to tell us four stories about the war, incidents that 'should have killed him'."

It was horrifying. "These things never leave you," he said.

Ed was good friends with my uncle, Jim Marietta, and helped me identify Morris "Sparkie" McFarland in the photo of the men together before the war. He shed a lot of light on my questions about Jim's experiences at the Battle of the Bulge, when his battalion was captured, receiving the Presidential Citation.

"The German's took their weapons, tied them up, standing, lined them up and drove by when they felt like it, randomly shooting them, killing most."

Pvt. Oda A. Sillings, Jr. Hawaiin Islands, March 6, 1944.

P.F.C. Arnold M. Daniels, March, 12, 1944

Lt. W. S. Rafferty, England, March 31, 1944

Cpl. Bailey Bryner, April 2, 1944

Cpl. E. F. Hinebaugh, Anzio Beach Head, Italy, April 2, 1944.

Lt. Anna M. Abbey, 76th General Hospital, Somewhere in England, April 5, 1944. "It hardly seems possible that the boys I grew up with are grown men serving in Uncle Sam's Army all over the world. I know some of them are nearby but do not have their addresses. Could you send them to me? It would be so nice to see someone from home."

Loren J. Show, Norfolk Navy Yard, April 20, 1944.

Springer "Jack" N. Anderson, Staff Commander 3rd Amphibious Force F 1/c, Southwest Pacific, April 25, 1944.

P.F.C. Arnold M. Daniels, India, April 26, 1944
"Thanking you for the March *Chimes* and the pictures of Ohiopyle High School and Honor roll. I just heard that Billy Kurtz was killed in action. I hope not. Here where I am in India is very hot. I saw in the paper where some of the boys were griping about the camps they were in being pretty rough. Well, I have been through 36 of the states and any one of them would look good to me now, but take me back to Pennsylvania and I will stay the rest of my time there. Thanks again for the *Chimes*.

Cpl. Doran M. Ellis, Hawaiin Islands, April 29, 1944.

Pvt. Elwood Holliday, Rehabilitation Center (Brig), Camp Bowie, TX, May 1, 1944, "Listen, here is something to put in the *Chimes* if you send it to all the boys. 'Dear Friends, Just to let you know what a fool a guy can be, I have been in the Army 16 months. I thought I knew everything. So I took a longer vacation than my furlough called for. Then I end up with a general court marshal of which I was sentenced to 5 years and a dishonorable discharge. One thing about this Army, they give a man a chance to soldier out in 6 months. Take my word. Be back on time. Don't overstay your furlough. Not everybody gets the chance to soldier out so be careful. Your Friend, Elwood Holliday.'"

James A. King, Cox "A Swabby Till," Jacksonville, FL, May 3, 1944, "I will close with this one thought in mind, that you will keep Ohiopyle on the map for our returning."

Cpl. Elmer "Bud" Morrison, Europe, March 14, 1944.

Pvt. Herman Geska, Anzio Beach Head, Italy, May 19, 1944. "Just a line to let you know I am still all in one piece. I gained a few pounds, grew 3 inches taller, and am getting homelier every day but other-words I am coming along just fine."

John W. "Jack" Kurtz, Italy, May 25, 1944. "I am now somewhere in Italy. Have been in the service only a short time, but sure have traveled around. This place might have been a beautiful place before the war. Sure is an awful place now. Have received the news about my brother, Bill, being a prisoner of war somewhere in Germany. I sure am hoping and praying he returns in good health. I sure will miss swimming in the old river this summer. I don't care much for this salty water. Thanking you again for the *Chimes*."

Donald E. Harbaugh, Ft. Leonard, MO, May 28, 1944

P.F.C. Lewis Taylor, Hammond General Hospital, CA, March 28, 1944. "Palmer Thorpe was here but I didn't get to see him. About all the boys here are from overseas all shot up."

Pfc. Wendell Burnsworth, Camp Rucker, Al, June 15, 1944

Ray Wolfe S.C.3/c, Port Hueneme, CA, July 19, 1944. "I work in the Master Galley. We are equipped to serve 8,000 men although the largest has been only 6,000. To me that was enough."

Cpl. Herbert Shipley, Greenland, June 25, 1944. "I am glad to hear that Billy Kurtz is at least a Prisoner of War. It could have been worse. I sure hope Jack Cunningham will at least fare as good as Billy did." (There had been reports these men were killed before they were listed Prisoners of War). I (Marci McGuinness) tried for many years to get Bill Kurtz to talk about his experiences in a German prison camp. He laughed, 'I can tell you I ate a lot of rats.' He also said that if he was not blonde and blue eyed they would have killed him.

Pvt. John G. Cox, France, July 26, 1944, "I have received a copy of *Chimes* since I have come over to France. I sure like to hear about the boys from around home. Tell all the folks back there 'Hello' and their prayers mean a lot."

P.F.C. Melvin C. Bungard, Somewhere in Italy, July 29, 1944, "I visited Naples since I have been here. I am sure it was a nice place before the war. Am going to try and look up Fred Morrison in the near future, and hope I succeed in doing so. Tell "Judd" and the gang I said, 'Hello'."

Cpl. Warren D. Leonard, England, July 29, 1944, "Ray Shipley is in my company. We talk a lot of home and sure enjoy reading the *Messenger.* I located my brother, Elwood, about two months ago. We made plans to meet each other on last June 4th but as the invasion was getting so close, all 24 hour passes were canceled. We've given up hopes of seeing each other until after the war is over. My wife wrote and said he is in France now."

Sgt. James Williams, Hospital Plant, in Wales, August 3, 1944. "I just received my first copy of the *Messenger* today and want to thank you. I really enjoyed it very much. I am in the hospital recovering from wounds I received in Normandy. I will have to close at this time as I am not as strong as I once was and it takes a lot of energy to write being on your back." Jim passed away on a hospital ship in October, 1944, on his way home.

Sgt. R. W. Martin, Panama, August 8, 1944. "The news of the past few weeks has been very good. How long it will last is hard to say. It should end before Christmas in Europe."

L.J. Show, August 20, 1944, "I received the August *Messenger* a few days ago. It saddened me to hear of Wilmer Marker, and my cousin's deaths, and so many others wounded. I knew them all. A few days ago my barracks was a howling crowd of sailors. Now it is very quiet-they have all gone overseas. I am in a Ship Repair Unit but if I pass the Chief Carpenter's Mate examination, then they have to send me, too. It is good to receive the *Messenger*. It has more news than any newspaper could ever give."

P.F.C. Olaf Skinner, Wakeman General Hospital, Camp Atterbury, IN, August 24, 194. "I sure appreciate your kindness in sending the *Messenger* each month. I am caring for German prisoners now. I have had quite a bit of experience with Malaria fever and the treating of it on my ward."

Cpl. Harold Morrison, Siapan, Marianna Islands, September 30, 1944

"Just a few lines to thank you for the *Messenger*. I was sure sorry to hear about Pete Steadman. He was always a jolly person. I see in the paper also that a lot of the boys from there are down this way. If any of them ever get to this island I wish they would look me up. It has been quite a while since I have seen anyone from back there. I am glad to see that a lot of our boys are doing good. I only hope and pray they get home safe and soon."

A score of years later, the Morrison brothers are lucky to enjoy each others company.
L – R: Leroy, "Tug" and Harry.

Cpl. Doran M. Ellis, Hawaiin Islands, November 10, 1944.
"Yesterday I went to a U.S.O. Show."

Sgt. Louis Collins, France, December 5, 1944. "I hope this letter will find everyone in Ohiopyle in the finest health. I think I can speak for all the home town boys that your paper is a great morale builder. Thank you."

P.F.C. Forrest Martin, December 6, 1944. "When I was wounded I was first sent to Holland, then to Belgium, France, and ended up in England., having flown from Paris to southern England in a C-7. I only spent a month on the front."

Cpl. James R. Hochstettler, England, December 7, 1944. "The only one from home I have met here was Randall Hall. That was last Christmas Day. I saw him several times after that but he was soon off to France. It hardly seems possible we have been at war three years today. Many have lost their lives. It will be with deep sympathy to return home and not see these fellows."

Macdonald Morrison, New Guinea, December 9, 1944. "Just a line in regards of your booklet that I get about every month. I am very glad to see it. I know some of the boys who are away like myself. I read it all and give it to my buddies. We all have to read it. My name is Macdonald Morrison, address, Ohiopyle. I have been overseas 9 months on an island in New Guinea. This place is in the jungle. I sleep under a net to keep the mosquitoes away. I pray to get back by next Christmas if nothing happens. Love to hear from someone."

Cpl. Nettie C. Sproul, Ft. Bragg, NC, December 12, 1944.

G.E. Schaefer, S1/c, U.S.S, L.C.S December 15, 1944

Jesse Hall B.M. 2/c U.S.N., Ft. Emory Det., December 17, 1944

Cpl. E. F. Hinebaugh, Ft. Benning, GA, December 27, 1944

From:
3.0 4/10677

To:
MISS. LILLIAN Mc.CAN
ObioPyle
Pa.

CPL HAROLD MORRISON
ES G 14TH XMAS. AVKBN.
APO 244 % POSTMASTER
SAN FRANCISCO CALIF

Merry Xmas and
Happy New Year

— NOEL

From The Marianas
Your Friend Harold

1945

Cpl. Donald Burnsworth, Belgium, January 28, 1945. "Thank you for sending me the *Messenger*. My friends and I enjoy reading it very much. I hope the boys and myself can be back home before this year passes."

Cpl. Frederick C. Silbaugh, Belgium, January 28, 1945.

Pvt. Hampton Teets, Somewhere in France.

Dick DeBerry, France, January 30, 1945. "I am now in the mobile X-Ray unit here in France. Imagine my surprise the other day in the mess hall when I met my step-uncle, Pvt. Melvin Dean whom I hadn't seen for five years!"

Pvt. Ray E. Shipley, Luxembourg, February 7, 1945

Sgt. Kenneth Turner, Germany, February 14, 1945. "I am now in Germany, but I find the country here is much like Holland and France except that it is a little more destroyed. Each day brings us nearer to victory and home. Thank you for the paper and keep up the good work."

Pvt. Frank J. Hall, Fort McClellan, AL, February 17, 1945

P.F.C. James Helterbran, England, February 23, 1945. " You don't know how good it makes you feel to read something about the old home town."

Phillip Gosnell A/S, U.S.N. Hospital, N.Y, March 3, 1945. "Boy am I mad. I have Scarlet Fever. I was supposed to come home March 6 but just look now."

P.F.C. Arnold M. Daniels, M. Burma, March 14, 1945. "I sure hope I do not have to spend another year here. I would rather be back there in good old PA wading in the snow like the picture of Mill Run on the front page of the *Messenger*."

Pvt. James L. Jennings, New Hebrides, March 20, 1945, "You should see the coconut trees. That is all you see is big coconut orchards. We have our company right among a big grove. I have seen so many coconuts I believe I am beginning to look like one. I haven't met anyone from home here as of yet but am hoping to. Thanks again for the *Chimes.*"

Macdonald Morrison, Philippine Island, April 2, 1945

P.F.C. Arnold M. Daniels, M. Burma, April 6, 1945. "Not much I can say about Burma now, but included you will find a Japanese Rupee as a souvenir."

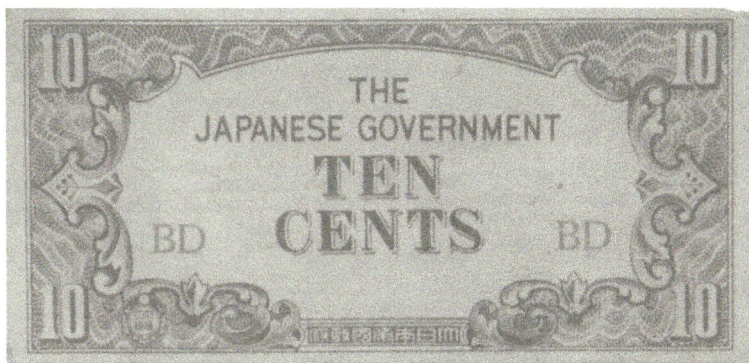

"Monroe" Daniels sent this to McCahan from Burma.

Macdonald Morrison, Philippine Island, April 12, 1945. "I get pretty lonely on this strange island."

Sgt. Calvin Darrow, Germany, July 14, 1945

Cpl. Arnold M. Daniels, Burma, July 16, 1945. "It will sure be a wonderful day when we all get home again to see our loved ones and friends."

P.F.C. Hampton Teets, Germany, July 18, 2012

P.F.C. James L. Jennings, I am somewhere in the Philippine Islands. Got here D Day plus two and it was a tough time. The town where I am was destroyed. All that's left is some buildings and a church. The Japanese treated these people terrible. Even took their clothing. They are in terrible shape. There is still fighting here so it is not too safe."

Sgt. R.S. McMahon, France, July 20, 1945. "We have had a lot of fun over here but I for one, like to confine my fun to the good old U.S.A."

Pvt. Tom Thorpe, China, July 26, 1945. "Thank you very, very much for the *Messenger*. I knew about every boy mentioned and am glad to hear they have done more than their part in the war. I hope to some day be back in those beautiful hills with most of those boys around beautiful Ohiopyle."

Pvt. Robert L. Hall, Camp Jos. T. Robinson, ARK, July 30, 1945, "How is everything on the old WM these days? Are you going to get a vacation this year or will it be like last? Next week we start bayonet drills."

P.F.C. Charles F. Davis, South Pacific, July 30, 1945. "About the boys we have lost in action, we all know that they did a good job, and that the good Lord will take care of them."

Cpl. Arnold M. Daniels, August 1, 1945.

Jesse Hall BM2c, Hawaiian Islands, August 7, 1945, "It sure is swell to know where all the gang is stationed. It will be great to get back to the mountains where I belong and take a dip in the river. Thank you for what you are doing for us."

Cpl. Herbert Shipley, Greenland, August 8, 1945. "Our main purpose here was putting planes through to England. Now we are bringing some of them back through here. Censorship here has been lifted so if you think of anything you would like to know about the country, just ask."

Pvt. Frank J. Hall, Panay, Phillipines, September 1, 1945. "There is a boy here from Confluence. Every time I receive the *Messenger*, he comes around to read it. I don't think I'll be here very long any more."

P.F.C. Kenneth Cole, Mindanao, September 13, 1945

Cpl. Arnold M. Daniels, Hell's Gate Assam, October 10, 1945. "I want to thank you and all the rest that kept the *Messenger* and *Chimes* going for us boys for it sure has been a big help to me to know where the boys are at over the world. I reckon this will be my last issue as I am soon supposed to sail for the good old U.S.A. Till then I will say thanks again."

Spring N. Anderson, F1/c, Philippines, October 17, 1945. "I guess there are quite a few fellows getting home on discharge isn't there? As for myself, I am a great believer in being home for my birthday in April."

P.F.C. Glenn R. Ravenscraft, Southampton, England, October 19, 1945. "Some of the boys here from other divisions said they had their toughest fighting from the Rhine River on up to Berlin, but they never put the 70th (my division) back on line again."

Phillip Gosnell, S2/c, U.S.N. Special Hospital, Palm Beach, FL, November 6, 1945. "Was glad to hear you are home from the hospital and feeling much better. It will take a little time to get your strength back but you will be good as new soon."

Ohiopyle Area Soldiers Lost in World War II

The
MESSENGER

VOLUME VI.   MAY, 1945   NUMBER 3

IN MEMORIAM

PRESIDENT FRANKLIN DELANO ROOSEVENT
Who died in the service of his country

ERNIE PYLE

Who told us things our boys had not the time nor permission to write. "I've hated the whole business just as much as you do who have suffered more. I've often wondered why I'm here at all, since I don't have to be, but I've found no answer anywhere short of insanity so I've quit thinking about it. But I'm glad to have been here."—Ernie Pyle

---

Cpl. Morris McFarland—Member of the air corps serving at Pearl Harbor when it was bombed, December 7, 1941; killed in action during the autumn of 1942, believed to have been shot down during the fighting at Port Moresby, New Guinea.

Dale Collins—Air corps radio operator serving in the South Pacific. Bomber and crew have been missing since a flight made during October, 1942.

James Bolen—Infantry, killed in action in North Africa during the winter of 1943

Eugene Steadman—Killed in action in France during July, 1944, in the bitter fighting that followed D Day.

Loren Collins—Killed in action in France in Patton's Third Army, Aug. 26, 1944.

M/Sgt. H. S. Weaver—Son of E. L. Weaver of Meadow Run, killed in action Sept. 19, 1944, while piloting a glider over Holland during the suicidal fighting that raged around Arnhem. He leaves a wife and thirteen-year-old daughter.

S/Sgt. James Williams—Fatally wounded while leading his men in Normandy during July, 1944, dying on a hospital ship en route home during October, 1944, buried in the graveyard of the Jersey Church near Confluence, Pennsylvania.

Pfc. Melvin Clive Bungard—Infantry in Italy and France, killed in action in Eastern France, October 25, 1944.

Harry Benton Cox—Son of Harry L. Cox of Keene, Ohio, grandson of Mrs. Savilla McLain of Ohiopyle, killed in action in Belgium in the armored forces during August, 1944. Harry was still in his teens.

Cpl. Ralph M. Burnworth—Air Corps gunner, killed in action during a raid on the Ploesti oil fields of Romania, a second attack made upon them on August 10, 1944. Ralph was the son of Walter Burnworth of the Hickman Chapel area and leaves a wife and child.

James G. Johnson, McMM 3/c—Aboard the USS Escolar, a submarine missing in the Pacific since October, 1944. Grandson of W. R. Johnson of Ohiopyle.

Wilmer Marker—Of Farmington, killed in action while serving in Italy with the paratroopers fighting in the Cassino and Anzio area during February, 1944.

Sanford Show—Of Farmington, son of Nelson Show, killed in action in Belgium during January, 1945, leaving a wife and baby daughter.

Harry Dale Hall—Of Hickman Chapel, killed in action in Germany while serving with the infantry, March 11, 1945.

I am printing the following June 1945 *Messenger* almost in its entirety. And bits from later issues. They report on the local men coming home from WWII, and those who did not.

The Messenger

is published in the interest of Christ and the Communities of Mill Run, Ohiopyle, and Hickman Chapel

Editor................................M. T. Hulihan
Ohiopyle, Penna.

Contributing Editor....Miss Lillian McCahan
Ohiopyle, Penna.

Mill Run Representative...Mrs. Ferne Work
Mill Run, Penna.

Hickman Chapel Representative...Ida Bailey
Mill Run, Penna.

time. The Scriptures are sufficient to direct men into the way of salvation. Moses and the prophets were sufficient for the Rich Man. In addition we have Christ Himself; also the record of what He taught and did, and the evidence of the power of the Gospel in the lives of men for nineteen centuries. If Moses and the prophets were sufficient in Christ's day, and those who rejected their message went to perdition, what will be the destiny of the men of our day who reject the testimony, accessable to all, and refuse to walk in the light that shines so brightly on their pathway? An eternal destiny of weal or woe awaits us, dependant upon the character we develop here.

May we be profited by the lessons of this parable and be rich toward God in every good word and work.

Rev. M. T. Hulihan.

HICKMAN CHAPEL BOYS
By Ida Bailey

This month we welcome home Dale Hay from Italy and say so long to Wade. Dale is home from fifty-five missions served over Europe. By some power this plane absorbed the heavy flak and held it, not allowing it to reach it's crew for any deadly work. Vienna, Leipsiz, etc, came within the bomber sights. I understand. After all this Dale presents a perfect specimen of manhood in every way. How proud we are of such boys! There is so much to tell this paper couldn't possibly print it all. We will just have to read between the lines. Wade will be inducted the last week of May.

Cecil Morrison writes that he was driving his jeep and trailer along, after leaving the load of shells and grenades at th'line, when an eighty-eight shell landed too close. A piece flew and hit him on the head, knocking him out. The Medic was trying to pull him from the wreck when he came to. Seven stitches in his head and fourteen in his leg resulted. He had been on the front line a month.

Cecil is back in, now, the ferrying squadron this time. He says he's not in love with front line duty—I guess not many are.

Joe Shockey wrote that he had the joy of eating some bread and jelly and drinking the coffee while yet hot that some Germans left rather hurriedly.

Wesley Burnsworth has been in a number of engagements on the Dashiell, beginning with Guan. I believe.

Marrel Taylor of the First Army, I believe, should be getting a thirty-day furlough before going on to the Pacific. Nelson Burnworth of Italy was OK at last report. Melvin Nicholson, reported missing, has now landed in the U. S. I hear. Willis Harbaugh is glad to hear of V Day in Europe, for that means help where he is in the Pacific.

From Germany, Orville Peck writes, he had the best seventeen-day pass he has had yet. Spent it in Belgium. May the fifth he said things looked good there. On the fifteenth Ralph Peck of the Engineers wrote that he was OK., had received a package from home which he enjoyed very much. Also had been able to get some chocolate ice cream, which sure was a treat. He's expecting to be sent to China.

Roy Van Sickle is expected home soon, being in the First Army. Signal photo cornsman Lee Stull in Germany seems to be doing well. At least he had the Germans goat. The picture his mother has shows him milking the goat in a Dresden china teapot while his Sergeant and two baby goats look on.

Our boys are fighting for freedom and humane treatment and men surrendering large armies, and old men like France's World War I hero, should receive consideration, I believe.

HICKMAN CHAPEL LETTERS

(Extracts from a letter to
Mrs. Hilary Burnworth)
U. S. S. Mindanao,
May 2, 1945.

Dear Mom,—

I'll bet it is nice up in the mountains now, isn't it? I always thought it was nice there in the spring and fall.

I am OK and getting along all right in the Navy but I sure am lonesome to see Hannah and little Nancy. I sure will be glad when this is over and we get to go back home to stay. I was sorry to hear about Harry Dale getting killed. I had a letter from Wesley the other day. He is OK but a little homesick, too, I guess. I am still doing light work and I can't work any place where it is too hot, but I'm getting along OK I can't seem to get used to this climate.

Love to all and may God bless you.

Your son, Hubert.
Hubert Burnsworth, S 1/c.

(Extracts from a Letter to
Mrs. Harry Hall)
Somewhere in Germany
April 26, 1945.

Dear Mother, Dad and Bobby,—

I just received a letter from Edna telling me about Harry Dale. It was a shock, although after being out here I can realize it. I am sure you are finding comfort in the Lord in these trying days.

Don't worry about me. I am O. K. It all seems so needless. We must keep our chins up and rely on the Almighty for strength and power to overcome the losses of this life. Soon we will all meet in the Great Life our Lord has prepared for us.

Love,

Your son, Bill.
Sgt. Wm. Mason.

Camp Pickett, Virginia

Dear Sir:

Am writing this letter to try to express my appreciation and thanks to all the friends and relatives that sent me cards, letters and presents on my birthday as they are too numerous to try to answer. They made this a wonderful day for me even though I am in a hospital recuperating from wounds I received in Germany.

I also want to thank all those who make the Messenger available for us boys in the service as it is a great morale builder.

I'll close for this time.

As ever,

Bill.

(William Scarlett)

Somewhere in Italy,
April 12, 1945.

Dear Ferne:

I suppose you will be surprised to hear from me. I'm not much at writing letters but here goes for a few lines.

I get the Messenger regularly and I appreciate it very much. I suppose Mill Run has changed some since I saw it last.

I guess we are pretty well represented on this side and also in the South Pacific. I have been over 300 days of combat and I guess I'm lucky I haven't been hit as yet.

Well space is running short so I'll sign off for now. So long and thanks for the Messenger.

Pfc. William Harbaugh

HICKMAN CHAPEL MISSION CIRCLE

Hickman Chapel Mission Circle met at the home of Ida Bailey, May 15th for White Cross work after the devotional and business session. The next meeting will be a covered dish dinner held at Mrs. Thelma Miller's June 19th. Following it will be the regular meeting.

The Hickman Chapel children will attend Vacation Bible School at Ohiopyle, Pa.

MILL RUN SOLDIERS

Ferne Work, Rella King and Ruth Minerd

As we go to press we can truthfully say we are happy for the great Victory that we have won in Europe but our hearts are still with those who fight on in the Great Vast Pacific.

S/Sgt. Dale Hay has the privilege of being the first hero from Mill Run to return in Massachusetts one week after Mother's Day. From Massachusetts he was assigned to Camp Meade, Md., where he was given his 30 day furlough papers. Dale served in Italy 7½ months as a nose gunner on a B-24. He has 35 missions to his credit.

Sgt. Sidney Prinkey a member of the 8th. Air Force ground crew was fortunate enough to have a 7 hour plane ride over Europe after V-E day. The boys were taken over battle scarred Europe to see what their planes had done toward the ending of the war.

Pfc. Fulford Sipe writes his father that his and Merle Taylor's Ordnance outfit (both are in the same outfit) was the first to take heavy equipment across the Rhine river on pontoon bridges and "Fifi" was the first of his outfit to drive a tank on the other side of the Rhine.

"Bobbie" Daniels spent a furlough with his family recently, then returned to Camp Upton, New York after being wounded and hospitalized. "Bobbie" surprised his mother greatly by his husky looking stature.

Jakie Basinger was home again on furlough telling of experiences in the Pacific of battles that he participated in. Richard Anderson was home on furlough after completing his boot training at Sampson, N. Y. Another Seaman James Friend spent a furlough with his family, Jimmie completed his boot training at Bainbridge, Md.

It may be interesting to Fulford Sipe, Merle Taylor, Bobbie Williams, and Joe Hensel that they all have the same APO numbers (230) via New York. We know Fifi and Merle are in the same ordnance outfit and Bobbie and Joe are in the Medical corps.

Donald Channing has been wounded the second time. Both times being slightly. His second wound was inflicted in Germany.

Harold King has been collecting souvenirs from Germany. He recently sent his wife and father different types of guns, a compas, and an ash tray made from a German shell.

William May has an APO via New York. Have not heard just where he is located. Two boys Frank Bigham Jr. and Glenn Work have been assigned to Florida. Glenn to Tyndall Field and Frank to an unknown camp to us. J. W. Hall recently landed in France and Ira Herman has been sent to the Pacific after serving 3 years in Corsica. Ralph Shearer left the third week of May for the service but at this time we do not know of his location.

Cablegrams and letters have told of the liberation of 3 soldiers who have been war prisoners of Germany. They are Melvin Nicholson, Clarence Hall and Robert Gallentine. Melvin's mother received word of his safety through a letter from him several days before Mother's Day. "Bob" Gallentine (Sammy Stickel's husband) was in American-British hands when he wrote. Clarence Hall said in a cablegram that he would be seeing his folks soon.

Delbert Minerd was serving with the 805th Inf. of the 77th. Division that was with Ernie Pyle when he fell. Delbert said they lost a great friend when Pyle was killed that he had done many things for them.

Roland Tissue is a Messenger and his name Cpl. Tissue is printed on his truck. Roland writes his mother that he expects to see them soon.

Eleanor Firestone has gone to Chanute Field, Illinois to visit her husband John who has been in the hospital for about 8 months.

We expect to see some of our boys back home before the next publication of the Messenger.

"Sam" Prinkey has arrived safely in England. He left the states sometime in March.

Wade Hay was inducted into the army several weeks ago.

Eddie Lowry of Connellsville known to many Mills Run boys is serving in the South Pacific with the United States Navy.

Mrs. Lester Harbaugh spent 10 days with her husband at Camp Blanding, Fla. Lester has recently been transferred to Fort Belvoir, Va.

V -E. DAY

The war in Europe has ended
And we are so thankful and glad
But when we think of the Pacific
Our hearts grow heavy and sad.

We know that our boys will win
But we know of the sacrifice too
So many must suffer and die
Before our boys there, will be through.

God grant that it soon will be over
When they too can lay down their arms,
For it isn't the will of our boys
To ever do anyone harm.

They are only there to protect us
And make our land happy and free
They have suffered and bled and died
For their country, for you and for me.

O, let us never forget them.
And never forget to pray.
That the Japanese too, will surrender
That, will really be Victory Day.

          —Laura Hewitt.

YEARLY REPORT OF THE SUNSHINE CLASS

Offerings .. $57.37 average per Sun. $1.14
Missions .. $17.86 average per Sun. .35
Attendance 315.
Visitors 39.
Visitors 43.

Filled a Russian war relief kit and gave $2.00 to the world emergency fund, and just recently gave $5.00 to the Connellsville Canteen.

OUR SOLDIERS
By Lillian McCahan

Word has been received by the parents of T/Sgt. Jack Cunningham and Sgt. Bill Kurtz that each has been released from a German prison camp and is coming home. We are anxiously awaiting their arrival.

Last word is that Lt. Roy Cunningham is still very ill. He was to have three operations for abdominal wounds and has not been heard from since before the second one. He was told he would get well but would never again be strong or able to do hard work. Never is a long, long time. As long as a man's life. Will we remember that long? Will we still remember and be kind when these boys are old men and much much younger generations strut the streets? Remember those words Maxwell Anderson put in George Washington's mouth? "This freedom will look easy by and by when no one has to die for it." But in a stricter sense freedom is never easy and we must always fight for it, and for the peace our boys are praying for. We can fight with other weapons than guns. We can fight with a typewriter, with a speech, in the pulpit, in an office where people come for just dealing. We will be taking a long step to peace when we realize that every people are entitled to their own country administered by themselves, even the Germans and the Japs. It will take patience and wisdom to work through all the bickering and win the peace but if we ask God's help we will eventually achieve it.

Speaking of the Cunninghams reminds me to tell you that the boys' Uncle Bill Rush, naval radio operator who has been a Japanese prisoner for so long, is still unheard from. Warren Cunningham, who has been in the thick of the infantry fighting in the Philippines, visited the camp where he was supposed to have been imprisoned, also other camps, but his name was not on the lists, which leaves but the slim hope that he may have been taken to Japan.

Ohiopyle was fortunate enough to have none of its Marines on Iwo Jima—though Lillian's Virginia cousin lost her husband there, leaving a girl wife and two small children—but Ohiopyle is well represented on Okinawa. Palmer Thorpe is there with the much-mentioned Seventh Division and Alfred Tressler is with the artillery. Chuck Davis, son of Russ Davis, and William Johnson, son of Attorney Johnson, are both on Okinawa with the Sixth Marines. They made the Easter Day landing Ernie Pyle wrote about and William spoke of Ernie's death in a letter home. And Bob Wolfe, of Kentuck, is another Marine on the island, and another boy with a nice family he hopes to get back to.

Lillian gets a thrill out of letters from far places and recently received one from 3. E Detling of Mill Run who is working in China with the Engineers on the Burma Road. Arnold Monroe Daniels of Ohiopyle and John H. Treacher of Farmington are also with the Engineers, both last heard from in Burma working on the Lido Road. Lewis Martin, radio operator on a transport plane, flies such distances it is hard for us to keep track of him—Philippines, New Guinea, perhaps Borneo. And I don't know exactly where Sgt. Andy Burnworth is except that he is in the Pacific area, thereby missing the big event of his married life, for his son, John Espy, was born this month. Charles Collins, in naval underwater detection work, was in Hawaii the last I heard and had met M. P. Frank Thorpe at a movie they both were attending. Frank has been in Hawaii so long I'm afraid he'll never be satisfied with Ohiopyle again. Jesse Hall, Jr., is in Hawaii now, too, with a landing outfit that seems to be

training for some tough naval landings. Another in the Pacific is Capt. W. R. Parsons, son-in-law of the Frank Baileys, one of the doctors attached to a hospital unit out there. His wife and young son are visiting in Ohiopyle this month. Paul Younkin, grandson of the Baileys, is still a naval cadet training in Melbourne, Florida.

Ralph Whipkey is home from Florida and I understand he is on his way to California. Jack Anderson got home from there, looking as though he had taken on some badly-needed weight, but blew in and out Bob Holt's store so fast Lillian couldn't finish her lunch quick enough to ask questions, but assumes our sailor is on his way somewhere important as is first class seaman Jack Kurtz. Another sailor home is Till King who came up from what so far has been a permanent station in Florida. And Paul Shay, who was wounded in the fighting in Germany, is home and his small brother reports him to be in pretty good shape.

Sgt. Ed Jackson, Jr., received the Bronze Star for his part in the artillery fighting in Germany. James Hochstettler's ordnance job has now been moved to Belgium. John Leonard has been sent to Europe, Delmar Holland and Glenn Ravenscraft are in Germany and I've just talked to Glenn's wife. Florence Morrison, into selling his dog back to WM.operator Shockey. Florence thinks a son is going to be enough to train. Mrs. Dave Collins received a Mother's Day card from the lieutenant of S/Sgt. Louis Collins who said he was glad he had Louis on his side.

Loren Walters came home the other day with a bride, an old girl friend he knew in Detroit. He has been stationed at Canute Field, Illinois, but like so many others is now on the move. I understand his brother, Jess of the Marines, is in the Pacific now. Sammy Dean landed in Infantry Replacement at Fort McClellan, Alabama, and Bobby Hall left this morning to enter the service after a year of excellent service to the Western Maryland Railway. That other railroad operator, Phil Gosnell, enjoyed his furlough home and is now back at Sampson, N. Y. And speaking of railroaders, I was surprised to bum a ride with a B. & O. one the other day and find he had received our Messenger a number of months while he was railroading in Iran. He, Clyde Tissue, is now discharged from the service.

Mrs. Myrna Truxal, widow of the former Methodist minister here, says her son was home on furlough and is now oversea. And Mrs. Chancey Tressler writes that her brother-in-law, Homer Tressler is in a port battalion in Italy and her husband, Chancey Tressler, is in the Infantry in the Pacific area.

Dear Miss McCahan,—

I think it is about time I wrote to all of you that are making it possible to send us boys the Messengers. I know it is sure something to look forward to. I want to thank everyone. I sure do enjoy reading the other boys 'letters and to know what part of the world they are in. I have been in quite a few places in the Pacific. I never thought it was this big. I can't say anything about this place where I am at the present time. I see in the Messenger that there are quite a few boys out here, but I haven't been able to find any of them as yet. Miss McCahan, I will close for this time, thanking you all again for The Messenger.

As ever,
Earl Richard Hall, I/c.

U. S. S. Oakland
April 28, 1945.

Dear Miss McCahan,—

Just a few lines to let you know that I have received two copies of the most welcome issue of the Messenger and was very glad to receive it, as it leaves a fellow know how the rest of the boys are getting along and where they are and that means a lot to us, as there are three of us boys on here from around there, and some of the other boys on the ship like to read that kind of thing.

Well me and my shipmates want to thank you very much for sending it to us and wish that we were there to help you out with it—mailing out so many letters to so many different people. Well, there is nothing else to write about and so I will sign off and hope to hear from you soon.

As a friend,
David W. Wallace, S 2/c,
Somewhere in Pacific.

Philippines
May 6, 1945.

Dear Lillian,—

I received the February issue of The Messenger the other day and certainly was glad to get it. A few weeks ago I received two issues of it but at the time we were too busy to write any letters.

We have been relieved and are in a rest camp now and it certainly is nice after spending such a long time in combat, however I'm afraid it won't last long.

I'm sending mother a commendation my regiment received. I'm not allowed to tell you where I am but it tells of one of our campaigns. The first one I was ever in.

The war news is much better and it looks like this war over here might be over before most of us anticipated.

Thank you very much and all those re-

sponsible for The Messenger, it's a great morale builder and I always look forward to getting it.

That's about all the news so I'll say goodbye and good luck.

Sincerely,
Warren.
Cpl. Warren Cunningham.

April 16, 1945.

Greetings,—

I am writing this letter from our billet; a German apartment house. They—the occupants—moved out and we moved in. We seldom stay longer than one night, so it don't inconvenience them too much.

This is the part of Germany where the people are true to the Third Reich. Slave laborers work in the factories and on the farms. They line the roads and cheer us on as we pass by. They fight like kids for a cigarette butt or a piece of candy. Usually they have wine and cognac they have taken from the Germans and they pass it on to us. By the labels on the bottles we can see that most of it is loot from France.

This is a nice country. Nearly all is farm land. There seems to be plenty of space but it is not wasted like some of the land at home. The land is green with a patch of woods here and there. The most popular crop seems to be sugar beets and potatoes.

Running out of time and things to write about.

So long,
Forrest.
Pfc. Maxwell F. Martin.

MEMORIAL

We pay tribute today to those who are
    far away
Some on foreign soil—others just now on
    their way
For those who've paid so dearly—made
    the supreme sacrifice
We petition God's mercy—the gift of
    eternal life.

The gold stars are scattered among the
    silver and the blue
Denoting loss of lads who died for the
    Red, White and Blue
Their names need not be mentioned—
    next of kin—perhaps it's YOU
Are grief-stricken but proud—of these
    sons who died for you. . .

We pay to them our homage—we respect
    and cherish too
The memories of their presence here—
    of things they planned to do

never see any it will be too soon.

I have showed this book to my friends and they all think it is swell that some-one back home thought of the boys over here.

You know I was never much of a church man but you will see a change in me when you see me again. After swet-ting out German 88s in the bulge you change a lot. I cannot tell you just where I am but I am near the Rhine with the 9th. Army, 84th. Division.

Please forgive this letter if you can-not read all of it but I have not been in shape to write much although I haven't lost a single day of combat.

I wish to thank all of you for this fine book and I hope to see you all soon. I have run out of words so I will close for now hoping to hear from you soon.
Your friend,
Ralph Marietta.

Germany
April 3, 1945.
Dear Friends:
Just a few lines to let you know I am still kicking.

I have been reading The Messenger and I like it very much although I don't get much time to read these days because we are choking Jerries. I have been in Eur-ope 7 months now and have been in com-bat most of the time. I thank God for my safety so far. I was in the battle of the Bulge. It was a rugged fight. I am now in Germany I was one of the first to cross the Rhine. Now we are still chas-ing Jerries. They are getting hard to find. It is like hunting rabbits back on the farm.

We are hoping that the war over here will soon end so we can come home for a few days I am a machine gunner in the infantry. I have many Jerries to my credit. I think of home every day. Pray for me and my buddies. We need the prayers of you folks back home. I saw a sign and it says "this is the road to U. S. A." but the road goes through Ber-lin and then to the U. S. A. I hope to travel this road the rest of the way. My friend who has been with me all the way says to pray for him too. Right now he is eating a box of "K" rations. He is from North Carolina, boy, he is a chow hound. I suppose you have heard him sing over the radio, his name is Pfc. Harry M. Denson. He also reads The Messen-ger. We are fox hole buddies.

We thank you for your wonderful work you are doing for us over here. I am also adding a little poem from our boys over here. This is it.

Tell all my friends hello,
We have fought a long way
And we haven't gote much farther to go,

Some day when peace and righteousness
by CHRIST is ushered in
Thru God's great plan of redemption —
all men shall live again . . .
—Pleasant Jennings.

A PLAQUE

A plaque stands proudly in the town's best square.
The bearer of names of men who've play-fair,
Heroes unsung whose record is there.
Who knows what they did that won't show there!
Many forfeited their lives that we may share
A world purred of evil, of bloodshed and care.
—Pleasant Jennings.

ODE TO A GRANDSON

A baby lies sleeping, his face so dear,
Small image of his father who isn't here,
God spare the grown one till victory's won.
God bless this wee one—my son's son.
—Pleasant Jennings.

CORRECTIONS

In my May memorial list I spoke of Cpl. Ralph M. Burnworth, who was killed in a flight over the Romanian oil fields. Ralph correct rank was that of Ser-geant.

And a line was left off of Mrs. John-son's poem, "Killed In Action," so I am reprinting the last stanza, which can cer-tainly bear repeating.
"We can only pray harder for peace soon to be
To a war-stricken world on both sides of the sea,
And bow our head patiently while the time flies,
Till God shall wipe the tears from our eyes."

Somewhere In Germany,
March 22, 1945.
Dear Ferne

I got a copy of The Messenger from you today and you will never know how hap-py I was to hear from the folks back home. The issue was of February and it had a lot of things in it that was very interest-ing. I have read every page over and ov-er again. I sure hope it keeps on coming each month.

I know my friends in the South Pacific would like to have some snow but if I

The MESSENGER

VOLUME VI   AUGUST, 1945   NUMBER 6

OUR SOLDIERS
BY LILLIAN McCAHAN

Our boys are coming home, one by one, some for thirty-day furloughs, some for shorter ones before they head for the Pacific. Howard Sarver of Sugar Loaf who was in the 342nd Infantry and Albert Lowry, Jr. who was in the 341st got home for their thirty days about the same time, and seem to be spending most of it on their farms. Then came Ray Shipley and Sgt. Warren Leonard of the 838th Ordance, both of whom were with Patton, and both looking well. Warren was in to see me with wife Freida and their small daughter and, like many other soldiers thought that, after all, the Lord had blessed Gernany with the nicest land, even though they haven't made it serve Him. They always say England is a nice country, too, but too backward.

One boy I haven't seen is Emerson Teets but he is here and is discharged from service. Emerson of the Artillery spent a good three years in Hawaii and other Pacific islands. And another boy home is Richard DeBerry. Dick getting thirty days on the farm before he begins treating the ills of the Pacific soldiers. I saw him the other day with his blonde girl friend, complaining that his dad was making him pitch hay. Dick was with a mobile X-Ray unit in Europe and said he x-rayed many hundreds, of every nationality, soldiers and civilians alike.

Phil Gosnell got home twenty-four hours, in much better shape, and expects to get home again this week before he goes South for further naval training. T/Sgt. Willie Martin came up from South Carolina for eighteen days before heading for the Pacific in a low altitude bomber. He enjoyed every minute of it and Lillian helped him enjoy part of them since she sort of claims part interest in this WM operator. Willie had another radio operator with him, a Joe Alexander from Leisinring. They will go to the Pacific together as replacements. Willie is the only one of the four Martins to hold a Distinguished Flying Cross but he is also the only one to receive five furloughs in three years. Dick, Willie, and Lewis all have Air Medals, the letter their mother received about Lewis's being in the Messenger. As I read it I thought there ought to be some medal to give the Infantry and Artillery who conquered Okinawa. Fel-

lows like Cpl. Alfred Tressler and Pfc. Palmer Thorpe who were tormented with mud, mosquitoes, and Japs till they could neither rest day nor night. The youngest Martin, Forrest, has a medal, too, but having been in the Infantry, his is a Purple Heart. His dad says he got his the hard way.

Another boy home is Dean Jackson who was with a port battalion in New Guinea and the Phillipines, having been brought back to US because of rheumatic fever. Dean said he was so sick he never knew when he landed in the USA. And another boy who should be here today is Pfc. Bill Holt, from the Quartermaster School at Camp Lee, who has passed all tests for the Pacific and may be sent that way soon. Will tell you more about that next month. Scion Burnworth, air corps cook, has been sent to the Pacific, and his nephew Kenneth Shipley is also oversea but I don't have his address yet.

A couple of disappointed boys were Walter McFarland and Carl Lewis. Both were held for the army of occupation. Walter's mother was looking forward to seeing for the first time Walter's baby daughter and Carl was looking forward to seeing his second son, a husky fellow he has never seen. Carl is with a medical unit in Scotland now.

Another soldier who rushed into town and out again was Sgt. Andy Burnworth who had started across the Pacific but was allowed to come home again because of the serious illness of his wife. She is better now and Andy is once more on his way. I would like to say to Andy's wife, and to others terribly worried, to have faith in the future, to ask for the Lord's protection and know that He does all things for the best as much as it is possible in a stubborn, warring world. I heard a story recently in another town of a mother whose only son was oversea, serving as an air corps mechanic, which we don't, after all, consider such a dangerous job. But she worried herself crazy about what might happen to him, and the tragic thing that actually happened was that the boy came back but had no home to come to because his mother was insane. I like to think our little Messenger has had a part in keeping such things from happening here.

To get back on a happier note, Sgt. Bill Kurtz was married last week to a pretty

The Messenger

is published in the interest of Christ and
the Communities of Mill Run, Ohiopyle,
and Hickman Chapel

Editor_____M. T. Hulihan
        Ohiopyle, Penna.

Contributing Editor___Miss Lillian McCahan
        Ohiopyle, Penna.

Mill Run Representative__Mrs. Ferne Work
        Mill Run, Penna.

Hickman Chapel Representative__Ida Bailey
        Mill Run, Penna.

young lady I don't happen to know. Our war prisoners have done pretty well for themselves since they arrived. Bill's brother-in-law, Ralph Whipkey, is in Hawaii now and got to see Frank Thrope and is hoping to see Charles Collins and Jesse Hall who seem to be at Pearl Harbor.

"Till" King, BM 1/c—not the promotion —was in Shomaker, California, for a while where Jack Anderson, F 1/c, is stationed, but Till went to sea before I could get Jack his address. Jim Gamble of the combat engineers has gone oversea on the Pacific side, too. Staff Sgt. Clarence Potter is still at Camp Ord, Calif. Capt. W. R. Parsons, son-in-law of the Baileys, who is working in a large hospital near Manilla, recently learned that he has a new daughter, born in Little Rock, Ark., where his wife, the former Roberta Bailey, is living. Bob Hall is nearby sweating out his basic training. Loren Waters is at Sheppard Field, Texas, and I understand he is learning to fly a helicopter. That's an idea Ohiopyle might be able to use when the war is over.

James McCartney, MM 3/c, is another boy who was called home just as he was ready to sail. He an T/Sgt. Walter McCartney were called home to Uniontown because of the very serious illness of their mother, but Bobby and Wayne are in Europe and, thus far, have been unable to come. Mrs. Ross Cunningham visited Lt. Roy Cunningham who is now in a hospital in Camp Pickett, Va. Billy Scarlett is there, too, both seriously injured, and Paul Shay is there with a less serious wound.

Paul Corristan, of a medical unit, writes from Lintz Austria, which he says is but a short distance from Hitler's birthplace, and he doesn't see why the people ever put up with him. Herman Geska is still in Italy. You and Lt. Bob Wildey have been over there so long, Herman, you ought to almost be naturalized. Staff Sgt. Kenneth Turner and his brother-in-law, Bill Wise, seem to be following each other around over Europe but never get to meet.

The youngest Thorpe, Donald, is in Camp Wheeler, Ga. for his basic training. Sgt. Bill Navoney, grandson of Bill Jackson, is at Salina, Kansas. Pfc. Dorothy Sproul is in the signal corps at Fort Myers, Va., and her brother, Cpl. Robert J. Sproul, is still oversea in the European area. Both are children of Bob Sproul. I understand Sgt. Dale Sproul, son of Tom, has been discharged, and certainly deserves to be. Cpl. Fred Dean is now at Camp Butner, North Carolina. Robert Shipley of Stonerville is training for the Navy at Sampson, N. Y. and his older brother, Sgt. Ernest Shipley of the 79th Division is still in Europe. Louis Wable has joined the radio operator clan at Scott Field, Ill. It's a swell clan, Louis, and I'm sure you'll like air corps radio.

LETTERS

Camp Joseph T. Robinson, Ark.,
Sunday, July 1, 1945.

Greetings,—

Here it is Sunday in Arkansas and it is sure raining. It has rained all day and I have stayed in the hut almost all day.

Last week we were, as usual, very busy from morning to night and the weather is very hot. I find I can take it a little better now than I could when I first came. We were in the field a good bit of the time but had some classes in the company area. We fired our first weapon, the bazooka, which shoots a 12 inch rocket. Next week we start actual firing with a M I rifle.

Was glad to receive the Messenger and want to thank you for it.

        Bob Hall

Phillipines, July 2nd

Dear Miss McCahan,—

I have received the Messenger and was very glad to get it because I haven't been getting much mail lately and it has also told me a lot about the boys around there.

And I feel sorry about Phil being in the hospital. He's had a lot of bad luck and I hope he soon gets a break.

I am having a pretty good time on the island. The people are a little different but they aren't as dumb as they look. They are really smart and know how to get around.

Well, I'll have to close for this time and I want to thank you again for the Messenger.
        As ever, Frank.
(Pvt. Frank J. Hall)

Phillipines,
July 3, 1945

Dear Miss McCahan,—

A note of thanks to you and all those who make The Messenger possible. It is good to read of those whom we know, but I re-

Pvt. Ralph Whipkey, New Caledonia, September 22, 1945, "A few lines to let you know where I am. Away down here at the end of the world. I just got word that we are shipping out again Monday morning. I hope I can stay here. Some already went to the Fiji Islands and Guadalcanal. Thanking you very much for the *Messenger*."

P.F.C. Albert D. Lowry, Luzon, November 7, 1945, "Received the *Messenger* when we were in Germany and was sure glad to get it. I know most of the boys and it is great to see what outfit they are in. I don't know when I'll get home but I will hope for the best. Good bye and good luck."

Messenger, June 1946...

Cleanse Our Own Heart
Make Old Wrongs Right
Restore Our Own Soul
Lay Siege to Some Other Soul
Compile A Prayer List
Be Sure of the Cooperation of the Holy
   Spirit.

—Lillian

OUR SOLDIERS
By Lillian McCahan

Our boys are still being discharged. Richard Hall, James McCartney, Charles Collins, and David Wallace have recently been discharged from long services in the Navy in the Pacific. Paul Younkin, grandson of the Frank Baileys, is discharged from the Navy, too, after long training in Florida in naval aviation and some service in Hawaii. He is planning to go to college in Pittsburgh this fall. On the other hand, two of our younger sailors, Johnny Collins and Bobby Shipley, are on their way to sea in the Pacific. Bobby, brother of Ernest Shipley, got home before he headed westward.

Sam Dean is home on furlough from Kentucky, Lt. Roy Cunningham is home from a New York hospital, and Walter McFarland is home on furlough now. Glenn Ravenscraft was last heard from at Camp Kilmer, N. J. Sturgeon McCartney has been sent to Fort McClellan, Alabama, for infantry training. Herbert Sproul, younger brother of Dale, was trained in the signal corps at San Antonio, Texas, and expects to be sent oversea soon.

Mrs. John Mancha, an older of Tom Sproul's daughters, writes that her sister, former Sgt. Nettie Sproul of the WAC's, now is working for the civil service in Baltimore. Mrs. Mancha spoke of her appreciation of the Messenger and of Rev. Wortman and Mrs. Estelle Jackson who were dear friends. I received a letter the other day from Sgt. Dorothy Sproul, daughter of Bob Sproul, who is in 17th Sig. Service Co., South Post, Fort Myer, Virginia, and the letter contained five dollars for the Messenger. Many thanks Dorothy, we need it.

Bob Hall writes from Wiesloch, Germany,

34

1947

Cpl. A.W. McCartney, Baguio Luzon, October 12, 1947, "By the time you receive this I will be moving again, yep, to good old Uniontown and Ohiopyle. I have waited a long time for this and will be very very glad to get home. Possibly soon everyone will be home comparing stories."

The Ohiopyle Honor Roll was erected in 1944 in front of the

Ohiopyle School. It was updated at the end of the war.

Note: McCahan has changed some of the actual names of the Ohiopyle folks she writes about in the following book. The Holts owned the stores. Some folks she just dropped their last names. I did not change this.

That Little Town

Lillian McCahan

Her story began on September 16, 1946...

I noticed one tree turned yellow today, one tree against a whole green mountain of them. The mountain rises beyond the river in front of me and even higher to the side. The gray Western Maryland Railway station where I am the agent sits above the river with our tracks crossing it at the end of the station platform. The Baltimore and Ohio Railroad tracks run along its opposite bank. Behind the station is our little town. They say the population of our little town is four hundred. You would certainly have to include all the small children and babies to arrive at that total. Looking down from Mason's hilltop farm it is a cluster of white houses in a spot in the canyon the river follows through the precipitous hills of Western Pennsylvania. Looking down, purple shadows come early in the green canyon on a summer afternoon, and the river is a shining ribbon on the bottom with a railroad track on either side till it comes to our town. At the street bridge the river bends sharply and flows three miles around a peninsula of land called Ferncliff Park before it rejoins the railroads in the canyon. The river slides in rapids beside Commercial Street and plunges over a falls at the end of it. Then it broadens out and flows smoothly past Long Rocks and Mr. Bremer's lodge. At the base of a tall peak it bends back and flows behind Ferncliff to the canyon, alternating in shallows and still pools, sandy beach and gray rocks, between the hemlock-topped cliffs of the park and the steep, wooded hills. At one spot it rushes through a gorge so narrow you can almost jump across it, then widens into a still, green pool that on an October day, when the trees around it are colored, is breathtaking with beauty. A smooth boulder shaped like a settee along the gorge invites lounging to absorb nature's peace beside the noisy stream.

Ferncliff is a forest with a picnic ground at the entrance. There are a hundred acres of tall, straight trees. Luxuriant ferns, rhododendron, and ground pine cover the foot of leaf mold on the forest's floor. White honeysuckle grows out of the gray boulders along the river where it flows behind the park. Back there a pheasant will fly up with a startling beat of wings, cross caw shrilly, while a squirrel leaps from limb to limb.

But the entrance of the park tells the story of the problem we face here. Back in the 1890s and the early 1900s our town was a popular summer resort. A white hotel built along the lines of a colonial mansion stood in the entrance of Ferncliff. There was a dancing pavilion, a fountain and flowers, and a boardwalk to the B&O station with lighted arches over it. It is all gone, torn down or rotted. Steep paths into the forest are washed out, low ones marshy and over-grown. Everywhere is an air of decay. Our town slipped off the resort map and into the depression and lethargy so gradually no one could name the date it happened. It's just that our old folks look around and see ancient, crumbling buildings, ashes and rubbish, along the river bank where once there were pleasant homes and rambler roses; note that the one hotel left lives on its barroom trade with mountaineers; that the summer boarder vanished with the horse and buggy in favor of the Sunday automobilist; that the small industrial plants that once furnished the town employment no longer exist. They realize their town is not keeping up with the times. But they are old, and they don't know what to do about it.

Even so, Ferncliff still serves the public, and so do the Lockes and Jim Robinson. Bob Locke's general store stands on the best corner of Commercial Street beside the Western Maryland railroad bridge and sells everything from sandwiches to washing machines. Bob is a stout man with boundless energy who looks fifty but is actually seventy. He meets regular customers, summer visitors and railroad men with equal gusto and that line, when troubled with shortages, about being just out today but there is a carload coming in tomorrow. His younger brother, Charlie, has a larger and more modern store beside him and competition is so keen between the men they haven't spoken for years. Charlie has made his son, young Bill, his junior partner, and Bob employs his nephew, Wes Locke, for his senior clerk. The young man's favorite sport is to get the exclusive sale of the best-selling product in town, be it a tastier sandwich meat, a new brand of canned goods, or the latest type of radio. The townsfolk crack many a joke about it. When Stanley Mason found Bob minus a girl clerk last spring he remarked,

"Easy tell young bill's coming back from the army."

"Why?" Bob asked warily.

"You seem to be getting ready for hard times. I see you laid off one of your clerks."

There's a story in town, too, about the time Bob extended credit to a struggling young minister, expecting to be paid when the congregation made up the preacher's salary. The young man and his wife, however, left town cheerfully after receiving their wages to accept a call in another town without bothering to stop at Bob's. Mae Locke, Bob's stylish stout wife, was aghast.

"And he seemed just as innocent as a lamb!" she exclaimed.

"Lamb! Lamb!" Bob growled as he cut steaks off a hindquarter of beef. "I was the lamb. I was the one who got fleeced."

Which disproves the accusation made the time Bob fell into an excavation and sprained his ankle. "My god! My god!" Bob groaned. Folks said his elder brother, old Bill, looked down sarcastically and asked, "Why don't you call on the devil? You serve him the rest of the week."

Bob and Charlie serve the public, good or bad, from seven in the morning till nine at night. And down at the other end of the street, where the river pours over the falls, Jim Robinson keeps much the same schedule in his combination service station, store, and lunchroom. He and Bob also open for the Sunday trade that rolls into town during the heat of the summer to swim in the river and picnic in the shade of Ferncliff. In spite of the crying need for improved accommodations for them, the Sunday trade continues to be an important business here and Bob and Jim serve them as best they can.

Our Sunday visitors come from the bare mining towns that cover all of our county except this remote corner back in the mountains. They come from the County Seat, the Railroad Center, and the other industrial towns where the best from the cement pavements hits you in the face during dog days. They even come from the bare hills and the roaring furnaces of Pittsburgh, fifty miles distant.

Our little town is a retreat for these workers who cannot afford expensive vacations. Hot Sunday afternoons they shout in delight as they leap into green water and feel its coolness ripple over their bodies. When the sun goes down their autos turn homeward reluctantly. Some linger over a campfire in Ferncliff or build one in the crevices of Long Rocks, the stone dock that extends into the deep, smooth water below the falls. Supper can be eaten down there in the shadow of a dark mountain jutted up against a rose-colored sky. And often young groups stay long after the evening star has come out above the peak and a church bell has summoned all the townsfolk who will heed to an evening service.

October 2, 1946

Winter and tragedy burst upon us Monday with equal sadness. Sunday had the warmth of late summer. But black clouds came out of the northwest on the wings of a cold wind as I ate my supper in my home in the Railroad Center and my aunt drove me back to this little town through a vicious rain. Fog and darkness closed in as we climbed the mountain. One could see only the white line in the middle of the road. She dropped me and my suitcase off at Squire Woodward's and hurried back to the larger town.

Frank Woodward is our eight-three-year-old justice of peace. He and his frail wife, Flora, live on the corner above the WM station, and I rent their spare bedroom over the Squire's office. It is a new house that the old folks moved in eight years ago to celebrate their golden wedding anniversary, one of the dozen in town with furnace and bath. Their only child, Lee, and his wife, Ella, live katy-cornered across the street, over between the Wolfe's and the Orndorff's. The Squire has a livestock farm up on Sugar Loaf that he drives to each morning in his pickup truck – though Lee has to drive it in and out of the garage for him. Squire Woodward is a small, sturdy, busy, sensible man, and living with him and his quiet wife has been a pleasure. They are the kind of people who attend to their own business and treat everyone alike. The Squire is a leading member of the Grange and the Odd Fellows, the president of the school board, and a trustee of the Methodist Church. Flora Woodward has prepared the bread and the wine for the Methodist communion service more years than many housewives here remember. I arrived in time Sunday evening to go to church with them.

A chill wind was blowing when I arose the next morning at six-thirty. Grey clouds alternately spit rain, sleet, and an occasional snowflake. I hurried down to the kitchen where the Squire had a fire in the coal range and the tea kettle hot. I ate a quick breakfast and ran to the station to build a fire there.

The morning was almost passed when I saw Mae Locke coming across the station platform and knew something was wrong. The men always attend to the freight business. She came in breathless. She said Harry Thompson had called their store from River Junction and told them to tell Ella Woodward that Lee had been hurt and was in the hospital and to come right away. Harry and Lee worked on a B&O track gang, and I knew the same thought was in Mae's mind as shot through mine – when men like that say "right away" – Mae verified my surmise by explaining that she had tried not make the news sound so bad. She said she had gone to both Ella's home and Flora Woodward's and told each that Lee was hurt a little bit and Ella was to go to the hospital. Ella had sent her to me with the request that I call Neil Turner, her brother-in-law who is the WM signal maintainer, to drive the car.

Neil was several miles east bonding new rail as the track-man laid them. But I knew Warren Martin, the B&O agent, had a son, Lewis, at home that day so I called the B&O station instead, a new fear nagging at my mind. Mr. Martin's youngest son, lanky young Forrest just out the Infantry with a Purple Heart, was the operator at the B&O tower that morning. Could he have caused the accident?

Mr. Martin said, yes, Lewis would come to drive the car. No, he didn't know the particulars of the accident. He'd just gotten word in the last ten minutes that it had happened.

I ran up to the Squire's and found Mrs. Woodward alone, trembling, silent tears running down her cheeks. The Squire had gone to his farm directly after breakfast and was not planning to return till suppertime. Lee had brought their dirty clothes over before he went to work. Ella and Mrs. Woodward had just finished washing the laundry for the two families and hung it on a line in the yard. Ella had gone home for a bite of lunch. I explained about Lewis and ran across the street to tell Ella. Ella's eyes were big, but she was trying to be calm as she combed the blonde curl she always pinned her hair into on top of her head.

I ran back to the station, then up to the garage after I saw Lewis pass. Mrs. Woodward and I stood together as he backed the car out, the old lady's thin body wrapped in a sweater. The clouds seemed lower and darker and the wind cut through us.

"You're not going?" I questioned.

"No," she answered in her low voice. "I'm so nervous I can't get dressed."

I ran back to the station, discovered the time was 11:30 a.m. and asked off for lunch. I went up to my room and made my bed and powdered my nose. Goldie Little from across the street took down the Woodward clothes. She, too, was worried since her husband worked on the same gang. I explained to Mrs. Woodward that I would go down to Ray Wolfe's restaurant and eat my lunch and then I would telephone the hospital. Ella should be able to tell us something by then.

The news had preceded me at the restaurant but no one knew anything definite except that Ray's wife's brother, Friday Daniels, had been hurt, too. I went to Bob Locke's store and checked with Wes, but he explained that Harry had phoned them very little. I called the hospital. The man's voice was hesitant. He said the doctor was working on Lee Woodward. I gave him the station's number and told him to tell Ella to call. I went back to Mrs. Woodward before returning to the station to promise I would have news in just a little bit.

No one called. The forty-five minutes between the time I went back on duty and the time I was certain Mr. Martin would be back from lunch seemed endless. Finally I called the B&O station.

Mr. Martin said, no, a train hadn't hit the motor car.

I breathed a sign of relief. Then Lee wasn't cut up by an engine. And Forrest didn't cause it.

Mr. Martin said it seemed the men were riding on a push truck hauled by a motor car and the truck had derailed. One man had a leg and arm broken, one was hurt about the head. That was all he could find out.

I ran up to Mrs. Woodward's with the news.

"If Lee just has a leg and arm broken, they will heal," I pointed out hopefully. "Or if he just isn't hurt too bad about the head."

"Yes," she agreed longingly, "if it just isn't too bad."

She had folded the clean clothes and was ironing the un-starched ones to ease the awful suspense and make the time pass quicker.

"We'll just have to wait," I said. "We can't disturb the doctor."

"Yes," she answered softly, "but it's so hard to wait.

I never knew just exactly how long she had to wait. I was afraid to leave my office for fear I'd miss the phone call, which did not come. At 4 p.m. I was getting goodnight from the train dispatcher. Gwen Waters, a tall, athletic woman, came in and told me that Lewis had returned from River Junction, gotten the Squire on Sugar Loaf and taken him and Mrs. Woodward to the big hospital in the County Seat where Lee had been moved. She said Ella had gone with Lee in the ambulance when they transferred him to the larger hospital and that Lee was bad hurt, his head crushed in.

I found the Woodward home unlocked. The fire was out in the kitchen stove, but it was still warm, the oven door open, and a white shirt Mrs. Woodward had ironed hung on a chair in front of it to be thoroughly dried. I thought it was the Squire's and let it hang. I took down the ironing board, took the other ironed clothes upstairs, and got dressed for supper.

After supper I wandered about aimlessly, to the Martins, to Charlie Locke's, down to Neil's. Neil said his wife was with Ella at the hospital. I got my canvas gloves and some paper at the station and returned to the Woodward kitchen and built a fire. A fire helps some, and lights, and hot water. Ella's big yellow tom cat went in with me from the cold, dark house across the street.

"All right," I told him, "we'll keep house together."

Tom retreated under the kitchen stove until the fire was going good, then settled himself on the cushion of the kitchen rocker. The teakettle began to sing, and I sat it back. I left tom sleeping and went out and down the street to the weather-beaten home of Mrs. Wolfe.

Katherine Wolfe came from Scotland with her parents when she was six to a farm on Greenbrier Mountain. Now she is seventy, a stout, motherly woman who walks with a cane and who has tended the sick and laid out the dead in every home along her street. Her daughter, Isabel, is almost as stout as her mother, teaches the one-room Kentuck school on the top of that same Greenbrier mountain, and can always be counted on as a friend. It was natural to turn to the Wolfes, to sit in the old rocker in front of the fireplace while Mrs. Wolfe talked quietly of death and how one must be strong to meet it. After a while, Ella's brother, Tack Corristan, came in and said that Neil's wife had phoned at last and said that Lee was dying. His head was beginning to swell. Lewis was bringing the old folks home.

I hurried back to the Squire's. Neil soon came, too, explaining that he would take the car when Lewis brought it and drive to the bus line for David, who was on his way home from Baltimore. David is Lee's only child, just out of the army and but a few weeks on a new job.

After an interval of silent waiting we heard the car and opened the door. Stout, gray-haired Bess Bailey whose home is opposite Ella's was leading Mrs. Woodward. The Squire was walking behind them. It was the first time I had ever seen him defeated, slow, bowed, completely without vigor and the will to go on. He just sat down. Mrs. Woodward was shaking with cold. She clung to my hand, tears wet on her cheeks. Then she went into the kitchen saying she believed something warm to drink would make her feel better. She took off her hat and coat and went to the stove. The white shirt still hung on the chair before the oven door. A sob wracked her body as she lifted it to the table and began to fold it.

"Well, Lee won't need his shirt," she wept. "I ironed it."

After a bit she made herself some instant Postum® and sat down and drank it. Lee was the only child she had succeeded in raising, all of the others having died when they were children. The Squire had often told me about his little daughter who had died when she was six. He said he had always thought she was the brightest and prettiest little girl in town. She had died in his arms of scarlet fever.

"Six children," Mrs. Woodward despaired over her Postum®, "and all of them gone."

But even in her tears she seemed the bravest of the couple. In the back of her mind was the simple thought that there was going to be a lot to do and she must try to keep well to do it. Isabel came in. She, Bess and I sat down with the Squire in his office. We tried to think of something to say but couldn't. Mrs. Woodward came in and sat down with us.

"I wish," she said, "I could have heard what that doctor told Ella."

"Well, I can tell you," the Squire said slowly, "he didn't give her any encouragement at all."

He sighed. "Oh, I never wanted the fellow to work on the railroad. He could have cut mine props on the farm and made as good a living. But of course men get hurt doing that, too."

We knew it was hard for him not to harbor regrets. He had hoped Lee would take an interest in his livestock farm, but Lee had preferred a bi-monthly paycheck. Through many years of Lee's life the Squire had been superintendent of the Methodist Sunday School, only recently retiring in favor of Isabel. Lee, a shy fellow who dreaded any public show of emotions, seems to have never ventured to either Sunday school or church so far as anyone could remember. Worse still, in the Squire's eyes, he had been working on Sunday. The Squire believed in the strict rule that work should not be done on the Sabbath.

But Lee had not worked through choice. A new division engineer had come to the B&O, a driver rather than a leader. "These gangs must keep up to the schedule I have laid out for them. Make them work on Sunday. Any man who won't work on Sunday can't work for me on weekdays."

Meantime, young men who had spent three years in the Pacific or a couple in the meal-storm of Europe, and who had come back from the army with the expectation of going back to the track gang they had been drafted from, found their gang had been laid off. So they had been spending their time at the hotel bar, drinking up their twenty dollars a week unemployment insurance, while tired men were paid overtime for overwork. Had that anything to do with the accident? I wondered bitterly.

Bess's thoughts must have followed mine. She spoke of seeing Lee come home from work Sunday evening while she was entertaining guests on her porch. She said his feet had drug a little and there was a tired look on his face. He had joked with them about being the only working man in the crowd.

Bess and Isabel soon said goodnight, admonishing the old folks to go to bed and try to get some rest. They did. As Mrs. Woodward wound the alarm clock she was taking upstairs with her, she voiced our vain hope.

"If Lee would just rally in the night!"

1st Week of October

I heard the Squire go downstairs early the next morning. I watched the clock's hands on the stand beside me and got up soon afterward. While I was dressing, Mrs. Woodward asked to come in and get a tablecloth out of the bureau in my room.

"Mrs. Wolfe is down there," she explained as I opened the door.

"Did you hear anything?" I asked.

"Yes," she said, her voice breaking in a sob, "our boy is gone. He passed away at four o'clock."

I just said, "Oh."

I was glad the Squire was at Ella's while I was eating breakfast. Once I remarked that it looked like there had been a frost and Mrs. Woodward agreed that there seemed to be a light one on the roofs. Otherwise the aged mother did her work silently. Bess told me later that it was Mrs. Woodward's seventy-sixth birthday.

When I went back at noon one of the track gang had brought her Lee's cap and dinner bucket. She opened the bucket in my presence and sobbed again.

"Look! There's the poor boy's lunch!"

There it was, indeed. Two red tomatoes, Ella's sandwiches. and cake wrapped neatly in waxed paper. A man's head had been bashed in but there was not a wrinkle in the waxed paper about his sandwiches.

October 7, 1946

The remaining days of last week were a different kind of a nightmare. A nightmare of funeral plans, people, flowers, and a still, unfamiliar corpse. The funeral was set for Friday afternoon and in the meantime everyone who had ever known the Squire, his wife, or his son's wife, came to one house or the other. Lee's body was placed in Ella's parlor, with flowers banked to the ceiling. The Squire built a fire in the furnace to take the chill off his own parlor but after another light frost the sun came out again as warm as summer. The frosts had been too dry to kill and the flowers bloomed in the yards as prettily as ever. But the old Squire just sat with his head down. His truck was not moved out of his garage all week. Once, when ladies from the church told him he must accept it all as God's will, he answered falteringly,

"Flora and I are old. I would sooner it had been us. Lee was just in the prime of his life, only forty-seven."

The ladies were members of the Ladies Bible Class whose monthly social meeting I always attended, but I would have liked to have silenced them that day. I do not think Lee's death was God's will. I do not think any of the terrible things that happen in this world are God's will. I do believe the Lord takes care of His own when they ask His protection, but he does not change the course of a brick in mid-air to keep it from hitting the man below. As Sgt. Hugh Brodie of World War II wrote before he died in air combat,

"The vast unalterable way
From which the stars do not depart
May not be turned to stay
The bullet flying to my heart."

The Lord performed His miracles when He made us and gave us the complicated mechanisms that are our bodies. He performed His greatest miracles when He made the world, the rain, the sunshine, the growth of plants and humans. He gave us everything we need with which to have a long happy life if we manage it well, much as a father bequeaths an inheritance to a son that will provide him a living if he handles it wisely. But the Lord does not do the managing for us, and cannot be blamed for the things we do to ourselves, and to our brothers. Our wars and our accidents are of our own making. Our diseases and our early deaths from them come from our carelessness, and the fact we are often still groping in the dark for the knowledge to prevent them. The Lord has said, "There, Man, is your inheritance. Let's see what you will do with it."

I knew that the Squire believed all this, that he did not think God had a fiendish will, but it was not good for people to voice such thoughts now when he was so shaken. I feared, too, that he might be worried because of the impression given that Lee went to his Maker without a prayer. I did not dare tell him that the men said Lee prayed constantly between moans of pain. I did not want the old folks to know how much Lee suffered before he was drugged into the unconscious state he was in when they reached his side. But when I thought it over I decided the Squire was wise enough to know the truth without being told. I had seen his wisdom in his decisions regarding the rural and town folks who came to him night after night with their legal troubles. I knew he would understand his son's heart better than the others and know that Lee, in his own quiet, retiring way, held to the faith of his fathers. Lee, who always had a little smile, a little joke, was always thoughtful and uncritical of others. Perhaps Lee's measure of service in life would not have been considered enough for another, but it was enough for Lee. We do not all have the same talents. And I decided the Squire, who worked close to God up there on his farm, would understand.

An investigation of the accident was held in the B&O station across the river, and Mr. Martin told me it came to no definite conclusion. No one had seen exactly what had happened. Everyone was looking the other way, even the men who were thrown off the truck. It seemed Lee was riding on the front of the truck behind the motor car, perhaps on some boards. But another man sitting on the boards was still on them after the accident since the truck only derailed and did not upset. Friday Daniels was thrown off and was in the hospital – the man with the broken arm and leg. Remembering Lee's weariness we wondered if Lee had become dizzy and fallen off in front of the truck, pushing Friday off and derailing the truck as he fell. Or had the fall been caused by shifting boards and tools? We will never know.

Ella had been one of a large family, and her home was filled with well-dressed women and prosperous-looking men who had left our little town long ago and obviously had done well. They came from Pittsburgh, down from Buffalo, up from Georgia. Wednesday and Thursday evenings the townsfolk were added to these guests and there was scarcely space to move in any of Ella's downstairs rooms. People who had not seen each other for years shook hands and laughed and talked, in spite of their sympathy for the grief-stricken family. Only an occasion as heart-rending as this could have ever gotten them all together again.. They hadn't thought much about Lee in life but the account of his death in the newspapers of the County Seat and the Railroad Center made them realize how much they had always liked him. Or it brought to mind some service the old Squire had rendered them in the years past. They came to the house of death from all over the district.

The men gathered in the kitchen, glad to see each other after the years of separation, and couldn't resist the temptation to exchanging views on business and politics. Newcomers filed into the hushed parlor where Ella and Flora Woodward sat. They signed the register, looked at the flowers, but did not linger at the casket. No one would have recognized Lee. His abundant pompadour had been shaven for the x-rays and the shaven head was badly swollen. The face was mostly plastic surgery. Ella explained through her tears that it looked well in contrast to the way he had looked Monday night. The Methodist minister and his wife, the Rev and Mrs. Kooser, had come up from the Railroad Center and Mrs. Kooser suggested closing the casket and putting a good photograph on it.

"But I haven't got a photograph," Ella sobbed, "not a single photograph. Lee would never have his picture taken."

Flora Woodward sat quietly in Ella's parlor with her son's corpse both evenings and greeted visitors. The strain was eased by the comforting realization that so many cared, that they had so many friends. I could see the searing grief relaxing its clutches and once in a while she smiled when shaking hands with an old friend she had not met for a long time. You can't help being a little glad when you have a great many friends. The folks who crowded Ella's home those two days Lee laid a corpse succeeded in accomplishing what they had come to do. They succeeded in taking the terror out of Lee's death for those who were left behind.

Even the Squire looked better. He sat in Ella's dining room Thursday evening talking in a low voice to a tall, graying man.

"That's Mr. Baxter, one of his Grange friends," Bess whispered to me. "He lost a son in the war."

The Ladies Aid served a lunch in paper plates to guests and relatives at noon Friday. The funeral was at two. The day was very warm and sunny. The service was held in Ella's parlor and not nearly all of those who attended could get indoors. Both the porch and the front yard were filled with people who stood silently, trying to hear the service. The automobiles they had come in were lined on either side of the street from Ella's to the WM tracks. I ran up from the station between trains and stood across the street as Ella came out on the arm of David, the pale old couple following. The shiny black hat Ella had bought for the funeral was as small and perky as the hats she always wore, and her head was high, but her face was chalky. Somehow the proud way she held up twisted my heart more than if she had been weeping. They took Lee to Johnson's Chapel and buried him in a country church yard.

When they returned Mrs. Woodward helped with supper for her relatives at her house and Ella's sisters took over at the other home. Then most of the relatives said goodbye except for Ella's out-of-town brother and his wife, who stayed with her, and Mrs. Woodward's sister who stayed with the old folks. I sat in my station a while trying to read but by nine I realized I, too, was sick from the strain of watching the ordeal. I locked the station and went up to the Woodward's. The house was dark but the door was unlocked for me as usual. Upstairs the bedroom doors were closed, and I knew by the silence that the Woodwards were seeking healing in sleep.

2nd Week of October

The next day was a Saturday of heartbreaking beauty. Russets and ambers were coming out on the hills. On my way to lunch I noticed that Bernice Orndorff's maples had turned yellow while I wasn't looking and that the old maple that hung over the road at Bess Bailey's was yellowing, too. The sky was blue and sunny above them, and the air was balmy. It was a good day to be alive, the kind I sometimes whisper thanks to the Lord for allowing me to have, but Saturday I was thinking of the Squire.

Tack Corristan had come down that morning and taken the Squire's truck out of the garage for him, and the Squire had gone to his farm for the first time since he was called away from it on Monday. The beauty of the day and Lee's death would be mingled in his heavy thoughts. I knew the Squire, like myself, was a realist in spite of our Christian faith. We feel that the Lord knows His business, and we don't believe in making fools of ourselves by questioning His existence or intentions. We don't, however, know with any certainty what is in store for us after death except for the words of Jesus – "In my Father's house are many mansions – I go to prepare a place for you." We believe in trusting those words and not fearing death, for ourselves. Nevertheless life is good. And Lee was no longer here to live it.

October 9, 1946

There is always one day in October that the trees are more beautiful than all the others. That day this year was yesterday, October 8. The afternoon was warm when I closed the station at four, and my feet naturally turned to Ferncliff Park to see October's show at its height. There was brilliant red foliage interspersed between the green all the way along the riverbank, and two trees near the falls were the most beautifully blended shades of flame and gold it would be possible to create. I ran down into the park from the railroad tracks and turned out the old road that runs the length of Ferncliff. Leaves rustled under my feet. All the low saplings had turned bright yellow and cast a peculiar light under the tall trees towering above me that were changing their own color scheme. At the end of the road I went down to the riverbank and clamored over gray rocks to the gorge and the deep pool beyond. The hill that rose from the opposite bank was every shade of red and orange and the low bushes that grew by the river had all turned garnet with an occasional yellow spice-wood bearing yellow clusters of fringe-like bloom. I lay back on the rounded stone of the "settee" in the hazy, fading sunlight, smelling the clean air with the tang of autumn in it, listening to the white water rushing through the gorge. Then it was time to turn back and leave it all.

This evening rain fell slowly but had not yet spoiled perfection. I got away from the station in time to walk down to the falls and look at the colors of the park across the river, each tree a different shade. On the town side big yellow poplar leaves lay on the Stewart girl's green lawn. The rose of sumac beside their fence was deep wine. I went out to the arched bridge and looked down on Meadow Run, a shallow mirror between bright hillsides. I turned my gaze toward the river and saw that three of the maples down at Mr. Bremner's were still green, one green and red, one green and yellow, one flame and gold. The hydrangeas along his driveway were all tawny pink. I stood under my umbrella and let the beauty sink into me a while as automobiles splashed by and the rain fell more steadily. I descended the steps behind Castle Rock to the river to see how many more shades the trees on Ferncliff and the bushes growing in the rock of the riverbank had turned, but they were too blended to ever describe. Finally I turned back to Woodward's with wet feet.

Pleasant warmth greeted me when I entered the Squire's office. Mrs. Woodward and her sister were cooking supper in the kitchen beyond in anticipation of the Squire's arrival from Sugar Loaf. Upstairs I raised the shade of the window beside my bureau and looked out on the sunset while I dressed. I was thinking of God's autumn gift, the perishable beauty of the leaves, and of how man returned it with ugliness. The newspapers have been filled with private crimes and international brawling. There is prophecy that another world wide conflagration may burst out at any moment, though I knew, too, that people all over the world, little people like myself, were praying for peace. Could the war mongers look on beauty like this and still want to destroy? Why could they not lift their people's heads and bid them look at the good gifts around them instead of filling them full of hate? Such were my thoughts as I left Woodward's for supper, the rain falling softly on my umbrella in the gathering dusk. while I hurried across the bridge to the hotel where our discharged soldiers hung sullenly over their beer.

October 23, 1946

The leaves have clung through three idyllic weeks. Rain at the end of the first week dulled and softened the colors in the distances, but there were still bright reds and yellows on the low bushes by the river. The sharp, cool air was filled with the spicy odor of drying leaves. Late Sunday afternoon of that week a wan sun was setting behind the blend of russets, green, and gold, when my sister's family returned me here and tarried to look at the hills and smell the autumn. The chill from the river soon drove them back to their car. The next morning was clear and cold with a white frost. My zinnias by the station walk were frozen, which only made the lemon and gold of calendulas show up all the prettier. Each morning after that there was a brisk white frost, a pink sunrise, and warmth in the late afternoon when I went for walks through the rustling leaves.

Now the trees are browning but there is still much yellow on the hills and red on low sumacs against the bank of the B&O railroad. Pink, yellow and white chrysanthemums are blooming in Mrs. Chitester's yard, which I see through the clean windows and freshly laundered curtains of my bedroom. Mrs. Woodward hired Goldie Little to help her with fall cleaning and they have just finished the upstairs. The Squire is slowly cutting the dried stalks of his sweet corn in the garden. The sun is hazy and there is an aroma of burning leaves where housewives have set them afire in little piles along the street. At dusk, when I go for supper, there is a streak of their blue smoke drifting above Ferncliff against the far hill, which looms up in the shadows a black silhouette against the opal sky.

There have been two wedding showers this month for high school girl graduates married to discharged soldiers, home-town boys who have seen far places and are glad to be back from them. The older girl married a sailor whose letter to me during the war I well remember: "I never knew the Pacific was so big 'til I came out here." We published a church paper here those days, financed by the donations of the townsfolk, that we mailed free to our one hundred and fifty servicemen, and I put a column in each month telling them the news of home, what part of the service and the world their buddies were located.

Last Wednesday evening the shower was for Sarah Lou who married a staff sergeant of a battalion of the 99th Division that had won a presidential citation for their part in the Battle of the Bulge. The bridegroom's name again brought excerpts of letters to mind, of the Germans he had had to kill, of a bullet that went through his coat, of his restlessness in Germany after the war was over and his glum forecast that if he didn't get home soon he'd be back to a private.

Sarah Lou and her sergeant were unable to find a vacant house and have rented rooms in the hotel. The hotel stands behind shade trees and a lawn that reaches to the railroad tracks opposite the B&O station. The leaves were yellow and most of them on the grass the evening we arrived for the shower. Relatives of the wedding couple had obtained permission to hold the affair in the hotel parlor and dining room, and a long table in the dining room was soon piled with tissue-wrapped presents. Townsfolk gathered in groups to talk while the younger generation danced to the tunes of a jukebox. Lunch was served the assemblage in paper plates. Then the bride and groom opened their presents and found an electric toaster, iron, lamps, blankets and sets of dishes. The town truly wishes the sergeant well.

I walked out to Walker's mine yesterday and loved every minute of the hurried four-mile trip. R.H. Walker is a dark, silent man who keeps the store across the river where the post office is located. He had a coal-loading dock on the end of my station siding and a small mine a couple of miles out in the hills. To reach it you climb the hill from Meadow Run, with that peak at the river's bend in all its bright autumn hues looking down at you. Then you turn off on a dusty road beside Cucumber Creek that leads you to Stonersville. Stonersville is a dozen houses built on a flat place in the hills and surrounded by a second-growth forest. A few families, crowded out of our town or looking for cheap rent, occupy the best houses, which were built twenty years ago by a coal company who had ambitious plans that didn't materialize. A big, unusual-looking pine stands guard above the village. Walker's road crosses the creek there and follows a fence row 'til you come face to face with a mountain.

The dusty road I traversed was flanked with color, the fence row was garnet with sumac, and the mountain that confronted me was splashed with many wild hues. Walker's bin and the trestle that led from it to the mine were a rough affair, but I was impressed with the amount of work that had been done by so few men. Walker employs a half dozen men at his mine and none of them were there yesterday. They had filled their bin, filled their mine cars, pushed them out on the trestle, and had gone home 'til I got them some coal hoppers to load their coal in. All of the east wants coal hoppers this fall, and I have to coax them out of my chief, two by two. One for Walker, one for Mason, who has a coal-loading dock on the station siding beside Walker's.

Walker's mine, I knew, was but three feet, but it looked lower when I climbed to the entrances. Men got down on their hunkers and crawled into this hole in the mountain? I knew they dug coal sitting down or laying on their stomach, that they pushed their cars out laboriously as they crawled out, themselves. However, I had never actually seen the reason Walker loaded only two fifty-ton hoppers a week whereas Mason, who hauled his coal out of a six-foot mine with ponies, loaded three cars a day. I stopped and looked inside the miniature tunnel. The mere thought of crawling inside it made me shiver. I was very close to the earth on that lonely mountain but the men who dug Walker's coal get closer than I ever want to be. They fully earn their ten dollars a day, which they spend at Walker's store, in beer parlors, and on rattle-trap automobiles. Mason disdains them as undependable Maple Summiters, "work today and drunk tomorrow." Maple Summit is a lonely stretch of mountain road between our town and River Junction. There is a one-room school up there, and a weather-beaten church sits along the road lit on Sunday evenings with oil lamps.

October 29, 1946

We seem beset by sickness and death this fall. The Methodist and Baptist ministers have been kept busy conducting funeral services. There was gray-haired Mrs. Rafferty who left five sons doing well in the world, and an old fellow out at Stonerville who wouldn't have cared to have given too close an account of his. There was a young wife out in the country who committed suicide by shooting herself. No one knew why. There was our fifty-year-old trackman who had stomach trouble for years but didn't think he should go to the doctor for such a trivial matter. There was young Tressler from Maple Summit who died of diabetes.

Tressler had been guilty of more than one escapade. He was very tall and his disease made him very thin. During the summer of 1945 he borrowed a returned soldier's uniform and represented himself to the Red Cross in the Railroad Center as a soldier just released from a German prison. He succeeded in getting substantial financial help. The town got a smothered laugh out of the story, but they sobered when told he was dead. When I came back from the Railroad Center the Sunday of his funeral, I was told that only Elsie Tressler's old Ford and the preacher's automobile followed him to the graveyard. Elsie is a good natured sister-in-law.

Last Friday there was still another funeral. The Methodist buried Gene Simpson's wife, and the town sobered again from a much longer laugh than any snicker ever cast at Tressler. Gene Simpson had come from a home of the slum class. Though there is room here, fresh air, water, and milk and sunshine, for those who know how to make use of them, Gene's mother died of tuberculosis,. Gene was turned down by the Army because of symptoms of the disease. A brother who fought valiantly in Germany through the winter of 1944-45 came down with it, too, and is now undergoing treatment in a veteran's hospital. Never-the-less, a young widow, the mother of three bright boys, married Gene, and the romance has kept the town amused for the last five years.

Until the couple began going together no one had paid much attention to either of them. After that we couldn't help noticing, because we were always seeing them walking along the streets or the road with their arms around each other. Gene's a thin, sallow fellow who seldom talks, and we wondered why the widow had picked him, but later we heard she said he reminded her of her first husband. Gene bought a new suit for his wedding, and the widow wore white satin. I don't know who married them, but we had no trouble learning the ceremony had been performed because a friend drove them up one street and down the other in his auto, honking the horn jubilantly. They had their photographs taken and published in the County Seat paper. Everyone marveled over how well they looked. Folks swore the bride wore her wedding dress, veil and all, to town three straight days before she laid it fondly away. I didn't laugh too much, thinking of how many other women would like to hold on to that moment a little longer if there were a way.

Thereafter the couple was literally inseparable. Every time we saw them coming to town they had their arms twined around each other, with the three bright boys walking behind looking a bit embarrassed. In all the five years since, they never appeared in public except with their arms entwined. In fact Gene didn't appear in public except with his bride. The only time anyone ever saw him without her was when he was at work on a B&O section gang. They bought a couple of old one-story houses over on the slag dump across the river, moved in the worse one and rented the other to a discharged soldier. The soldier had returned from Germany a technical sergeant of the 79th Division with the bright cords of two decorations on his uniform. He did his part in the defense of two villages that had been captured, lost, and recaptured, all in one flaming night. Decorations, however, do not keep off the rain, and the sergeant needed a home for himself, his wife and small daughter. Gene was smart enough to make a profit out of the sergeant's need, but, otherwise, the couple seemed to grow more and more listless and their home more dilapidated.

Only the bright boys seem to possess vitality. They delivered papers, cut grass, and raked leaves, to keep themselves in clothes. They attended school regularly, made exceptionally good grades and were always polite. Frank, the eldest, was a favorite of a nicey-nice high school teacher who taught here last winter. She gasped when I pointed out his home. But she said they must have a good mother, because they were always clean and their clothes neatly patched.

The townsfolk continued to snicker each time they saw Gene and his wife with their arms around each other. Once the snickers turned into raucous laughter from the loafers on Bob Locke's store porch, and I stopped to inquire the cause of their amusement.

"The love birds fell out," they guffawed. "When she got around the corner a piece she stopped and gave him a slap, then she made him put his arm around her again."

When I saw Gene alone in his old auto this month I didn't at first realize what I was seeing. A few days later folks told me his wife had died of tuberculosis in the County Seat hospital.

I sent Gene and the boys a sympathy card. After the Charlie Locke's had closed their store at nine the evening before the funeral, they drove their new Packard up to the home of the dead woman's parents, and I went along. Their ramshackle house consisted of two small rooms Their daughter's body lay in its casket in the front of them. The room was crowded with people. The dead woman was dressed in her white satin wedding gown and Amy Locke declared there was a half smile on her face, as though she was glad to have it on again. I didn't stare. I spoke to the boys and their grandparents, signed the register and went out. Gene, as usual, was wordless.

She was buried in the Methodist Church the following day. The white church is just across the street behind my station, sitting on a green lawn beneath an ancient oak. I could hear the singing and preaching through the open doors and windows. They told me that rain began to fall as Gene's wife was lowered into her grave. By nightfall a cold rain was drenching the earth, and as I came out of Charlie Locke's with a head of lettuce for the social meeting of the Ladies Bible Class, I passed Gene in the black rain.

"Thanks, Lillian," he whispered, his face contorted with grief.

At the class meeting that evening the treasurer reported we had spent all our funds for funeral flowers and were seven dollars in debt although we had sent to no home except where the Methodist minister had officiated.

Our little world emerged freshly-washed and clean-smelling the next morning, which was Saturday, and the sun rose brightly. David was home from Baltimore for his first weekend visit since his father's death, and Mrs. Woodward was trying to bustle at noon. The Squire looked more cheerful and said they were getting ready for a trip to the County Seat. In the afternoon I was told Gene's wife's parents, the Tissues, were going to give their daughter's three sons a home till they could fend for themselves. The home would of course be those two rooms we had visited, already occupied by two of three of their youngest, half-grown children.

October 31, 1946

The Squire was up before six yesterday morning to meet a trucker who arrived with a double-decked truck to take a load of the Squire's lambs to market at Pittsburgh. They returned well satisfied as I was dressing for supper. The Squire said he had sold them for the highest price he had ever received for lambs in all his years of farming.

It was six in the evening, almost dark, warm as a summer night. I hurried to my office to learn the whereabouts of the evening local freight before I ventured across the river. At the back waiting room window I paused. It framed the ancient oak on the Methodist lawn, now bare of leaves. The black limbs were a filigree through which shone the crescent moon hung on the darkening sky beside the high steeple of the white church.

At seven this morning I paused to open the same window. Lohr was walking by on his way to the barroom. Lohr has what everyone thinks they want, an income he doesn't have to work to earn. He is the middleman in the mine prop business here. He is already deteriorating from the town's leading citizen to the town drunk. His clothes were crumpled, he was wearing a three-days growth of beard. His face was red and flabby and his whole body seemed to be shivering. He stopped and looked at his withered hands, took a few steps and stopped again.

I turned quickly away. The "Reading Hot Shot" was on signal. It is a fast freight train composed entirely of loads for the Reading Railroad. The work train was following it and a westbound train was out of River Junction, both to take the siding at my station for the eastbound local freight which had to pick up three cars of coal off the station siding. Mason's truckers were trying to get another one loaded but weren't going to make it. Maintenance men were coming in with mail pieces of machinery to be billed to the division shops. I had some coal to bill, some mail of my own to get ready – reports to the division offices.

We send out reports on the local freight train because the WM has no passenger trains on this division. The automobiles have taken so much of the local passenger traffic that local passenger trains are no longer profitable. The B&O specializes on the long distance traffic. Its streamlined diesels wind through our town with no recognition of us except to sound a warning at the road crossing. That means I have neither tickets nor express to handle. Mr. Martin attends to that on the one local B&O passenger train per day. I have a cinch.

I was busy with reports regarding my cinch when I heard Mason's footsteps in the warehouse. The warehouse is long, and I keep the door at the far end one-third ajar when on duty for lookout. From there I can see what the truckers are doing along the station siding. Mason is a wide-shouldered, warm-hearted, temperamental fellow in his mid-thirties. It takes him a long minute to come through to my office door, and I can tell the mood he is in by his footsteps. If they are quick he has a lot of things to do. If they are quiet everything is working out all right. If they are heavy he is in a bad mood. This morning they were heavy, thump, thump, thump, thump, threatening to go through the boards. I looked up puzzled. He had enough hoppers, which had been switched correctly. Walker wasn't in his way, wasn't even loading. For once I thought everything was going all right.

He flung open the door, his eyes blazing, his hands full of papers.

"Look at that, Lillian! Look at that!" he demanded. "That's supposed to go in today," he stormed as I accommodatingly looked at what I didn't understand. "This is the end of the quarter. This is payday. The payroll's to make up, the withholding tax has to go in. They'll arrest you if you didn't. And Harry Thompson's drunk!"

"Drunk?" I echoed, remembering that Mason employed Harry to make up his twice a month payroll. "Why I didn't know Harry got drunk anymore?"

"Drunk!" Mason yelled, "and he's lost the slips. Leonard and I have been down there with him all morning. He don't know anything. There's a report goes in to Social Security. He always leaves everything till the last minute, now he don't have anything done. I saw Kenneth Show's report down there, too. It's not done. See that? See?"

I didn't see because I didn't know what the rows of figures all meant but I said I did anyway to be agreeable. He stormed out. I remembered that Leonard had a lumber mill at Farmington and Show a grocery store at Mill Run. I peered out the window. Leonard had taken Harry out of Mason's long, rusty auto and the two men were walking their accountant around in the air. Harry looked like a wild man. His clothes were awry, his eyes that of a crazed animal. Slowly I began to grin. The more I thought about Mason's and Leonard's predicament the more it tickled me. I sank back in my chair doubled up with laughter. Obviously the Social Security and the Internal Revenue offices would get no reports from Harry Thompson regarding Mason Coal Company, Leonard Lumber Company, and the Show Grocery today.

In the afternoon Mason's blondly beautiful wife, Kitty, phoned me that she had her husband's reports all made up, she hoped correctly, and if I saw him to tell him to come home and sign them. By that time both the morning trains and my grin had gone and I sat pondering over this whole liquor situation. It is a business I do not relish. And it is a business that is increasing rapidly, along with the ruination of our people. Back of it is the almighty dollar, and I have often wondered why the American people can't see that. They are so busy asserting their right to drink anything they please, regardless of what it does to them, that they have never stopped to realize in how many ways people growing richer and richer off a beverage that can be diluted again and again and still be potent enough to drug the drinker into insensibility. If there was that much profit in any other business the law would be looking into it. And if there was that much poison put in a food or drug the maker would be thrown into prison.

There has been a great deal of tommy-rot written about why men drink. The facts seem to be clear. The drunkard drinks because the alcohol he is used to makes him crave more alcohol. He might have begun the vicious circle because he was idle, had no interest in life, or was in some other kind of rut. Other men drink because it gives them a kick they can't seem to get in any other way. Women drink because they think that makes them sophisticated. They kid themselves into thinking they are making themselves more desirable. It never seems to occur to either sex that the only thing liquor does to them is to make them more or less disgusting, depending on their degree of drunkenness.

I have wondered, too, why anyone with a comfortable living would want to drug themselves into unconsciousness. Is not life as precious and interesting to them as it is to me? All of my regrets are over the life I have missed, the places I didn't get to go, the things I didn't get to do, the eighteen years of night work when life became just one long night. Life passes so quickly I want to be aware and enjoying every moment of it. Why is it these others want to waste their hours? And why would they want to injure their internal organs any more than they would want to slowly cut off their fingers, a little every day?

As for Harry, he had always said he only drank when he had nothing to do. However, he had remedied that during the war. He had gotten a job on a B&O track gang and had become the town's best accountant, constantly in demand for that sort of part-time work. He had also gotten himself elected to the school board and was serving as secretary for the town council. Furthermore he had taken up the hobby of raising chickens, which took up a lot of his time. And, finally, his old sweetheart, now a widow, had moved back to town and was filling any leisure time Harry had left for her. Harry's fall off the water wagon had apparently been caused by some other blow-up rather than too many idle moments.

November 1, 1946   Last night was Halloween. The high school students had sold all of us tickets to a masquerade dance to be held in the high school auditorium. A masquerade always makes me foolish, and it seems to affect a number of other folks here much the same except that our foolishness shows up in different ways. Mae Locke and the Alice Locke family, especially John and his sister Gwen, delight in looking silly. John was dressed last night like a simpering female, Gwen like a funny man, and Mae like a grotesque woman. I, on the other hand, always want to look pretty. All the beads and flowers good taste prevents me from wearing I can blossom out in on Halloween. City women can indulge this passion by wearing evening clothes, but I would look sillier than Mae did last night if I paraded down Commercial Street at nine in the evening in satin slippers and trailing gown when all the good citizens were going to bed. Halloween gives us our only chance to dress up.

But it had been so long since I had had the opportunity I couldn't find anything to dress in. I dug a black lace dress out of our trunk in the Railroad Center, which I hoped would make me look like a Spanish dancer, but it was much too narrow, and I was woefully short of accessories. The beautiful black scarf with the pink roses in it I had been saving for just such an occasion had disappeared. My mother thought she had given it away in some of the clothing drives. "Why?" I grumbled. "If they wanted to keep their heads warm some of those old faded scarves would have done just as good."

In fact I had a hard time being gay at all. As I was hurrying to the Squire's to get dressed I met Viola, a dark-haired mountain girl who attends high school and who lives with her ailing grandmother in the house below the station that is owned by the railroad company.

Viola had tears in her eyes. "Miss M--," she asked, "do you think it's a bad sign when a pigeon comes to your window three times?"

I knew she was thinking about her grandmother and hurriedly advised her not to worry. At the dance I found that the young people had not masked but had attended in their street clothes with the express purpose of dancing, leaving the masquerading to us older and sillier ones with whom, I soon learned, no man would dance because of our rigging. They did march us around the room to music, however, and awarded some prizes. A girl from Mill Run in a pink taffeta evening gown won the first prize. Consolation prizes were awarded a girl in a sailor's uniform, to Mae's distorted lady, and to a widow dressed in an ancient white lace dress with a red sash and a wide white hat.

The rest of the evening we sat and watched the young people dance. The two young ladies who were our new high school teachers had solved the dress problem most expertly of all. They came in blue jeans and sloppy-Joe shirts and danced with all the best-looking men. The widow and I, determined to have some fun, teamed up for the cake walk and won it, but she spoiled the fun for me by remarking, "Well, you're the last person I ever expected to dress up!"

I went home depressed. Memories of other remarks came back to me. The beautiful girl who came into my office, where I sat at my desk with the telegraph at my fingertips and two lines of telephones at my elbow, and exclaimed, "How lonely it must be here!" And the beauty who told me, "that seems such funny work for a girl!" And the bartender's response the time a male friend stopped at the hotel and asked if I was in the dining room. "That woman?" he asked incredulously. Apparently a lady agent is a freak.

I was still feeling low this morning. I gazed through a slow rain at hills that seemed to have become bare overnight, except for a few patches of brown, clinging leaves. Through trains passed quickly and left me sitting idle. Neither Mason nor Walker were loading coal because it was the first day of the small game hunting season, and their miners had laid off to hunt. I thought of the lonely months ahead with those bare hills before my windows to stare at. I pulled the semaphore levers to clear at lunch time and locked the station door, trying not to give way to the terrible loneliness that was sweeping over me.

Grace Hinebaugh was coming up the street, quick of walk and lithe of body. She waved to me, smiling under her umbrella. Grace had that same quick walk when she had married Funny and kissed him goodbye. He went off to war and made the long trek through North Africa with the 45th Division then lived through another terrible winter on the Anzio Beachhead. It had been hard to smile then but the smile was wide now.

"Good day for squirrels," she called.

I called back a laughing answer. Undoubtedly quiet, slender Funny was sneaking through wet leaves that wouldn't rustle to stalk the sort of prey he liked to shoot, and there would be squirrel and gayety for supper at the Hinebaugh's tonight.

I lifted my head and drew in a long breath of the cold night. It smelled of wet, dead leaves, and I realized it was a good smell – and that the hills were somewhere between blue-black and the darkest brown – and that the world looked like November.

November 6, 1946   The Squire and I had heard rumblings long before election day so we were not greatly surprised at what happened yesterday. Last winter I had watched the General Motors and General Electric strikes cut deep into the railroads' revenue as trains went by with short tonnage. Then the tonnage dwindled to almost nothing this spring in the latter weeks of the strike of the United Mine Workers. Regularly every two weeks throughout the summer, I had brought my embargo file up to date. I took out a handful of embargoes of strike-bound plants, whose workers had decided to go back to work, and put in another handful embargoing plants whose workers had just struck. By election day I was so tired of altercations I swore I, too, would vote Republican if it would break up the crazy wave of strikes. Obviously most other people felt the same way. Everywhere people were losing work, losing money, going in debt, sometimes losing their jobs permanently. The lack of revenue made it impossible for many employers to keep them, as a result of the feuding between capital and labor. Everybody was sick of it.

But there is little likelihood of neither I nor the Squire ever actually voting a straight Republican ticket. The Squire in particular is just naturally a party man. The evening before election he rushed about distributing campaign literature as peppy as his old self. He said John Snyder, local Democrat leader, had fallen down on the job of reaching the voters. I smiled at his energy, wishing Ella had an equal interest in life. Ella still sobbed when she talked of her personal affairs, a perfect housekeeper alone in a perfect house with no one to share it with her.

Election day dawned bright and cold with a sting of November wine. Mason and assistant signalman, Charlie Collins, stood in my office and watched the Republicans going down to the little unpainted building below the tracks which serves as the polls, the council chamber, and emergency jail. The Republicans are always in the majority here which keeps the Squire and I on the defensive. Of course they are all our friends, and we love them all dearly – except on election day. The Masons and the Collins have voted Republican as far back as anyone has a record of the families, and the two men counted the votes for their side as they watched the townsfolk filing into the election house. They were mostly women at that early hour and finally I saw Mrs. Wolfe coming, leaning on her cane, and pointed out a Democrat. Mason admitted one straggled in once in a while. Then they both went down to cast their own vote before any more Democrats beat them to it.

I would have preferred to have voted for men interested in the welfare of America, but one never knows what men are interested in. For the most part I could only be guided by party platforms. And, like the Squire, I'm a Democrat. We have seen too much monopoly in the past, too many rights downtrodden, too much depression. Now we have been seeing radical labor trying to domineer. It is hard to vote wisely. Consequently, I don't feel as badly as the Squire over the Republican victory I have been reading about in the newspapers this evening. I have never liked to see one party get too much power. It always makes tyrants out of the Republicans and fools out of the Democrats. There will be enough Republicans in Washington now to keep the Democrats straight, and vice versa. If the combination has enough sense to make the belligerent men who lead capital and labor sit down and work together, instead of trying to get ahead of each other, we may yet come into a sane post-war period.

November 12, 1946

Armistice Day is not a railroad holiday, but after I closed the station at four in the afternoon I had time for a walk down Commercial Street and beside the falls. The water was very clear in the river. The deep pool the falls pours into seemed a much darker green then in the summer, perhaps because of the darker colors surrounding it in the frail sun. The trees were bare. The ground had a thick carpet of brown leaves where the park came down to the river's edge on the opposite bank, the dark green of rhododendron bushes dotting it and banking the cliffs.

In the evening the most sincere citizens met in the school auditorium for a program to commemorate the day. There were only a half dozen soldiers present, all in civilian clothes, so that an outsider would not have known they were there. But it is not likely that I will ever forget who served in the armed forces from this little town, after mailing our monthly church paper to them for four years to every quarter of the globe. I still have their letters telling me how glad they were to get "The Messenger" and read my column of news of home and their buddies. Scared, lonely, homesick boys telling me how glad they were their hometown had not forgotten them.

There is one from Sgt. Jim Williams that "The Messenger" never did catch up with until he landed in a hospital in England with seven machine gun bullets in his abdomen after fighting his way from D Day up through Normandy to the Belgium border. It is a V letter thanking me for "The Messenger" and explaining he can't write much because he is still very weak. He died on a hospital ship bringing him home and is the only one of our soldiers thus far who lies in his home soil. They buried him in the churchyard of the Jersey church on the road to River Junction by the way of Maple Summit.

There is a letter from Sparkie McFarland, written from Pearl Harbor a month after the attack, telling me to keep the trains rolling and he'd keep the bombers flying. The Japs shot him down over Fort Moresby. There is one from Sparkie's nephew, Walter, writing "God bless you" from England because I put a photograph of a snowy Commercial Street on a Christmas Messenger – the street he hadn't laid eyes on for four years. He is home now with his English bride and their two-year-old daughter. There is one from a nineteen-year-old Marine after Guadalcanal – "This is an awful war, I never knew how awful until I got in it myself." He's married and living in New York now, his face fixed up with plastic surgery.

There is the letter Willie Martin wrote, returned from thirty missions over Germany as air corps radio operator and on the west coast waiting for embarkation for Japan. "I suppose I could avoid more combat duty if I pulled the old gag about a nervous condition, but that isn't my choice. As much as I hate the army I still think we've got to win. And the war won't be won by the bright boys whose only fighting is for a safe job. I like a safe job myself, of course. But the choice is to go ahead and fight or lay back and let someone else do it." He didn't have to go ahead the second time, the atom bomb dropped and made it unnecessary.

There was the letter Lt. Roy C-----'s mother showed me as he lay in a hospital in England, pierced all the way through, assuring his young wife he was going to get well. But it took too long, and they are now separated. Only he, of all of those, was present at the Armistice Day program, sitting far back, dressed in quiet gray.

There were others who crowded my memory as I sat in the uniform auditorium, though they were absent, too. Mason's black-sheep brother, "Oudie," who talked himself into an air corps gunner's job, though he was in his mid thirties. He was flown to North Africa in an unsteady ship its pilot dubbed the "Coughin' Coffin." Oudie flew more than fifty missions and personally broke up and downed a whole flock of Nazi planes. He had his own name and that of his ship's in many a newspaper. The ship was good copy. An unknown mechanic had written a prayer on the side of it before it left the States, perhaps because he could do nothing more for it on such short order. It was enough. Despite the heavy flak, no member of the crew was ever injured, even the day the Coffin was finally downed. Oudie came home with a row of medals to a big celebration, and to become a black sheep all over again.

I remembered Clyde Bungard picking his guitar and leading the gang's singing on the bench by the barber shop under a June moon. Harry Dale Hall strutting a little for the girls' benefit the last time he came to church, on his way to what to him was the fatal drive across the Rhine at Remagen. Pete Steadmen tagging after me, wistfully telling me how he was going to the army, hoping I would make a hero of him. But I never got around to it till he fell in Normandy. The letter Loren Collins wrote his mother as he followed Patton on the last Mother's Day he would ever see. What his cousin Dale told his folks on his last furlough before he headed for what was then the unequal struggle in the Pacific. "There won't be anything left of me but this identification tag." His plane was lost as the battle raged for the Solomons, so they didn't even find that. The letter Ralph Burnworth wrote his wife of the interesting places he had seen – before he flew over the Polesti oil fields.

The only way any of those could have taken part in the Armistice Day program was in the silence, while we thought of them in their graves. There were others not present, suffering from wounds or shock, who never wanted to see a uniform again. Thinking of all of them I wondered how we could possibly put on a program that would fittingly honor them.

We didn't. A band wasn't available, just a squeaky church orchestra that was a poor substitute. The ladies of the Legion auxiliary hadn't mimeographed the songs the audience was to sing, and we got mixed up in the stanzas, even of "America" and "The Star Spangled Banner." Certain older ladies, and myself, are always called on for "readings" when our women put on a program, but the old ladies keep getting older, and they had nothing in their repertoire that fitted the occasion. A younger mother did better by just giving a talk. The preacher's talk, however, was too long and not to the point.

Finally, it was my turn. I looked over the crowd and wished I could say something, or make them say something, that would somehow show our gratitude for the victory and commemorate the lives that had been lost; but I knew I couldn't. So I repeated Seeger's "I Have A Rendezvous With Death" and Rice's "Voices From the Dust" and sat down. The program ended with another song of which we didn't know all the words.

November 18, 1946   November has been a beautiful month, after all. Only that five minutes before I get up enough will power to crawl out of bed at 6:15 a.m. is hard. That five minutes after I have shut off the alarm and turned on the light and am very warm and snug in bed with the frosty air coming in the window and the dark graying with coming daylight. Once I have washed the sleep out of my eyes, ate my hurried breakfast and put on my suede jacket, I feel like singing. I run barefooted through thick, white frost with a pink sky above me and the mountains still dark against the dawn. The sun rises slowly while I stir up the banked fire in my burn-side stove. I can see its first red rays hit Mason's hilltop farm and then come down until sunlight has flooded the cold town.

By noon it has warmed the earth and taken the frost off the golden bloom of my marigolds and calendulas. But the cold comes back with the sunset, and I put a red jerkin and a brown tweed coat over my dress before I hurry to supper through the dusk. Always I look up at that blue-black mountain against the last streak of light as I hurry along. Its silent bulk has the power to ease away all anger, nerves, or worry. It seems to say, "This bitterness and fear is man-made and not very important, for the Lord God is always here."

November 23, 1946

It's hit us again. Another coal strike. This time it sprung on us in the night with no warning and no coal stored in anticipation of it. Tuesday morning, `9th, I was rushing about as usual, stirring up my fire, billing out the coal, getting my mail ready for the local east, when Mason called me. He said the B&O, where he ships half his output, would not move his coal. He wanted to know what the WM was going to do with the coal he had on its siding. I told him I was going to move it unless I got instructions to the contrary.

I got them within an hour. All coal on railroad sidings was frozen by order of the Solid Fuels Administration. I gave the local a highball to keep moving instead of stop flag.

Nobody knew what was next. The mines closed with the men in a disgusted mood. Five weeks till Christmas, business booming, a swell time to draw a couple of good pays, and John L. Lewis pulls a thing like this on them. Mason's miners were non-union, paid a little better than union wages to lure good ones, but there were a lot of things to be taken into consideration before any more cars were loaded.

First of all the coal had to be moved daily or there would be no room to put in more hoppers. I was told in a couple more hours that it could be moved to a storage yard. But with continued operation storage yards would get full, too. Then I was told the coal could be moved to its destination if the consignee had a permit. Obviously permits were the next things to go after if the mine was to operate. But if it did operate there would be danger from pickets. It would be cheaper for Mason to shut down and go hunting than run the risk of damage to his mine. He could hunt small game the rest of November, deer in December, go Christmas shopping and then settle down in his comfortable home to enjoy the holidays.

But Jim Williams couldn't. The father of the war hero, minus a foot he lost in a mining accident years ago, drew good wages in Mason's mine, but his last pay was all spent. There were thirteen mouths to feed up at his place, and he had planned to give them all a little Christmas. Jim wanted to work and so did a dozen other miners in similar financial circumstances.

For the rest of the week Mason was undecided. He would come in and ask if I had any hoppers coming for him, and when I would ask him if he wanted any, he would go out without answering. B&O agent Martin pointed out that Mason would hardly attempt to mine coal till he was sure it was not going to be held in a storage yard somewhere. He could not go on mining if there was no money coming in to meet his payroll. That fact was soon relayed from all small coal operators to their brokers, and the permits began to come through with the coal orders.

The small coal mines in the towns east of us began going to work. Each morning the chief dispatcher and the superintendent's clerk checked the line to learn which mines were working. I smiled to myself. Throughout the war the small deep mine that loaded by truck on team track or station siding was looked on with disdain. The strip mines, also loading by truck, were treated with more respect because their output was from ten to fifty cars per day instead of from two to four. They had more money and built their own sidings. Mason and Walker had but three car-lengths altogether on the station siding on which to place hoppers for loading, and railroad officials had made me the continual brunt of wise-cracks about my "mining business." The ten thousand dollars or so circulated in town monthly as a result of that business was important here because, before the war, WPA and relief checks were about the only thing circulating. In contrast, however, to the amount of money in exchange elsewhere on the WM, the mining business we small town agents were able to encourage on the vacant ends of our station sidings was good only for a length.

This time it was our turn to smile. Having our employers so interested in whether the small mines that loaded at our stations were or were not willing to work, really gave us a kick. Every dog has his day.

Mason finally decided last night to go back to work. I was loafing in front of my fire listening to the radio when the second track chief rang, thinking I might be spending the evening in just such a way. He said the Lehigh Valley car of coal I had was bunker coal that didn't need a permit and to get it moving. I called Mason to tell him the decision, and he retaliated that he had a permit for the other car, too, and for as many cars as he could load, and for me to get him some hoppers.

I relayed that information to the chief.

"If you're kiddin'," he razzed back, "I'll give you the same thing for Christmas I gave you last year!"

November 29, 1946

  While we have been worrying about the coal strike, the rest of November has slipped by. Last week more than the coal was frozen. There came a spasm of rain one dark dawn followed by a cold wind from the west end, and the next morning the ground was frozen hard, and my marigolds had given up trying to bloom and dropped their heads. Now they are only brown stalks from which I have cut the seed, leaving them stand to protect the new poppies, which have come up from seed during the fall and are tenaciously clinging to an inch of green leaves regardless of the weather.

  I ate Thanksgiving dinner with my family in the Railroad Center, returned here in the late afternoon and spent the evening with the Martins. There are five of the Martins at home, the B&O agent, his wife, and their three sons. The boys have all been discharged from the army within the past year and are working their way into regular jobs on the railroad. Richard, the eldest, a taller, better-looking edition of his dad, likes to talk about the two years he spent as air corps radio operator patrolling the sea between Panama and the Galapagos Islands. Lewis never talks about his stint as radio operator in a transport plane between such places as New Guinea, the Philippines and Japan. He just won't eat rice and spam. Forrest, the youngest, served the hard way, in the infantry, and is still wondering how he got back from Germany with nothing worse than a healed thigh wound.

As for Mr. Martin, he is ninety whole pounds of argument and kindness. He would give you the shirt off his back if you were in need and argue with you all night if you favored the political party he is against. His learned way of arguing, his straight little carriage, his eyeglasses and his clean but worn clothes, have given him a special nickname. The town calls him "Shakespeare." Like myself, he began working in his teens and has belonged to a labor union ever since. Unlike me, he was through the Philippines in the Spanish American war, and later blew glass, waited on tables, and sometimes worked as a common laborer all over the country before he settled down to be a railroad agent.

Mrs. Martin is the informal hostess of this group and does a good job of it. Her hair is white, and there are crinkly laugh lines around her eyes. There is always food and laughter at the Martins, which made it a good place to spend a holiday evening in our quiet little town that doesn't even have a motion picture theater.

The Martin's married daughter and their second son were absent from the family circle. The second son is Willie, who received his Distinguished Flying Cross for his thirty missions over Germany by mail because he wouldn't go through a ceremony to be awarded it. He is the real cause of me being so well acquainted with the Martins. I taught Willie telegraphy. Now he is working for the WM in their Cumberland terminal offices.

Willie became my student through no effort of mine. At the time, taking a nineteen-year-old into my office and devoting all my spare time to him was the least of my desires. However, there was no B&O telegraph office near then, Willie was determined to learn telegraphy, his dad was just as determined that he should have the chance, and they talked me into it. I protested vainly that I was only a ham who couldn't get rain water running down a spout. They didn't think it would matter. I was afraid it wouldn't. So I sat down and wrote out the Morse code, told Willie to get himself some dry batteries, and I'd bring up my old learner's instrument.

Teaching Willie turned out to be one of the most enlightening and satisfying experiences of my life. While I taught him Morse, the rule book, and what is expected of a railroad operator, he explained all manners of subjects to me. The mechanism of a camera, the life of a glassblower, how this, that, and the other is grown or made, and why. Not the least of what I learned was that I liked to teach. I found it fun to enlighten others. Training a green kid into a self-assured young fellow able to take over a job gave me the exhilarating feeling of having accomplished something. Willie now has become such an expert telegrapher that only politeness causes him to slow down to my speed.

But the bond between us was more than student and teacher. It was born that first week he practiced in my office. Standing behind him, gazing at the back of his slender neck and watching his long, slim fingers feel out his key and precisely, if slowly, pounding out each letter, my eyes suddenly filled with tears.

They were tears only a telegrapher's family could have understood. Mine has been one all the way back to before great uncle Ed Johnson boomed with Edison. Willie brought the past back to me, a past it would be hard to explain to one outside the clan. It would be necessary to know a telegrapher's heart, the things that matter to them and the thing that don't. You'd have to grow up with telegraphers as I did, know the kindness of the old dependables, the glamor and hard polish of the boomers. You'd have to be raised on their democratic philosophy regarding their fellowman, hear them spouting off radically about religion and politics, as this kid sometimes spouted off, and finally come to realize that they were not near as radical as they sounded. In fact the hard truth was that nothing ever mattered very much to them, not even the Hereafter, but whether or not they could get the stuff that came over their wire and could send it the way they wanted it sent.

Railroad operators can be made, but a real telegrapher is born. God alone knows why he is born! For we who have grown up in their families know too well how money, honor, and sometimes even ordinary comfort pass them by without them ever being conscious that they had missed anything. The only thing they made sure not to miss were the clicks of their sounder. Sam Morse invented more than a code and a means of transmitting it. He also fathered a new race of human beings, whom he probably died without ever learning about. As I watched Willie that day I realized he, too, was a born telegrapher.

My tears were memories. Memories of my father, whose philosophy of life this boy led. Memories of how he lived, and how he died, nerves shattered, worrying because he had forgotten an unimportant train order. Memories of the cynical crowd whose fingers this boy now practiced with, the show-offs who could take anything that came over a wire. Of how my father always felt inferior to them because his hands were too cramped for their perfect sending. Memories of all the old telegraphers I had known who have passed on. Now I was being privileged to develop a new one, and I wasn't sure I was doing him a favor.

Another fellow to sit at a telegraph table while life throbbed by outside beyond him. Another lonely one, on his sounder racing the financial news of the world he'd have no part in except to copy the figures. Willie and I have often quarreled since, argued over many a principle. Notwithstanding, Willie is the real reason I feel a little closer to the Martins than I do to the rest of the townsfolk.

November 30, 1946   This is the last day of small game season, a bright sunny day with lots of Western Pennsylvania people taking advantage of the weekend to get out in the woods. Both men and women, dressed in hunting clothes, were coming in Ray Wolfe's restaurant at noon for sandwiches and coffee. The fresh autumn air and the brown hills will be good medicine for them whether or not they cussed in shooting a squirrel or rabbit.

More important to me is a meeting scheduled for Monday. The Superintendent called yesterday and told me to have my coal shippers at the station at 10 a.m. for a talk with him. Both of them are threatening to load more cars per day and want more space. Also Bob Sproul, a farmer with land near Walker's, wants to open a mine. I sincerely hope a way can be found to build more track here, though it is a hard problem in this sharply-curving canyon. If there was a hundred feet more track on the entrance of my station siding we could get the full production of Mason's mine, instead of splitting it with the B&O, and could pick up some other revenue by giving another man a chance to mine his coal.

December 3, 1946

Snow began to fall Sunday, the very first day of December, and the thermometer fell with it. Monday dawned on a sleet and snow storm. I ran to the chilled station and began to build fires, carry out ashes, fill coal buckets, sweep, and dust in preparation for my official guests. The coal bin is in the warehouse, as is an axe, discarded wooden crates, and old newspapers. A fire in a Burnside is easy to make. You just punch a hole through the ashes so it can get it's breath, put the paper in the bottom, the wood on top of it, and the coal on top of the wood, light the paper and shut the door. After a while you open the door to keep the iron bowl melting.

The Superintendent called from his Cumberland office at eight to ask about the weather. I casually have told him it was snowing a little, about an inch on the ground. I could have told him there was an inch of ice under the snow, making hazardous driving, and it was growing colder by the minute. But I let him find that out for himself. Mason, Walker, and Sproul were keeping their appointment – Mason and Sproul's sons sacrificing the first day of deer hunting to be there – and I wanted my superintendent to meet them.

Shortly after ten I saw the nose of a familiar maroon sedan appear at the end of the station and hurried to the warehouse door. The Superintendent, accompanied by his assistant train-master and division freight agent, was looking over the seven-hopper-length siding that I had so often pleaded be lengthened to accommodate the coal shippers. He glanced over his shoulder at me banteringly.

"Fine day you picked."

"You picked that," I grinned.

The officials and the coal shippers gathered around the waiting room stove while I busied myself with monthly reports in the agent's office, listening to the conversation through the ticket window.

The Superintendent was still adamant. He would not lengthen the station siding at the entrance where the loading ramps had been built at the expense of several hundred dollars. The station siding branched off the passing siding and to lengthen it there meant changing both tracks. Unfortunately that was the only place it could be lengthened. The other end of it was against my station platform. That part of the short track lay along the street where the ground was smooth for trucks to back up to box cars and had to be kept for the occasional box car of lime or feed that was shipped into our town on the WM The entrance was rough, hilly land on which wooden docks had been built high enough to dump into a coal hopper. The coal shippers were willing to pay for more track there but the railroad's engineering department thought it unwise to change the switches.

The Superintendent said he would be more willing to tear the station down and lengthen the track across the station platform. That remark, I thought grimly, was made to aggravate me, not because he has any notion of doing it. However, he went on, he was not willing to do that at the present time. What he would be willing to do and thought the advisable thing would be to build a siding for the coal shippers east of the station where there used to be an old lumber siding. Of course the shippers would have to pay $6400 of the cost of the ties and rails, and they would have to bring in a bulldozer and grade down the road bed. He made no reference to what that would cost since that would be the shippers' problem, as would the cost of improving an old road to the proposed siding and installing some sort of dock or conveyer for loading coal.

I kept very still in my inner office, hoping my shippers would be able to see a way of accepting the Superintendent's offer though it sounded impossible to me. Their responses revealed to me that they felt the same way about it but didn't want to say no. The tall Superintendent was an imposing man, and they wanted to load coal on his railroad. They gave him guarded promises to think over the proposition and left.

The Superintendent came in my office, still full of banter. "You heard what I was going to do to your old station, didn't you?"

I ignored the taunt and began talking about the proposed siding. I prophesied my shippers wouldn't build it.

I was right. Mason came in today and told me he had a man estimate the cost of the grading and that it would be another $6000 by the time he improved the road and bought a conveyer. That would mean a cost of at least $12,000, only $6400 of which they could get back at the rate of two dollars a car – or in about three years of good business, if they had good business. The war was over, the future of coal uncertain. He pointed out that he could lengthen the B&O siding on its dead end another car-length for a hundred dollars, and it would be wiser for him not to load so much coal per day than to spend so much money. Walker had no reason to put any money in a siding. He had two car-lengths of room now and Mason's only worry was that Walker might cut him down to a car a day on the WM. Walker's dock, which was built first, was ahead of Mason's at the entrance, holding the two car lengths. Mason had but the one car length at his dock and could reach no more cars if Walker chose to load them. Thus far Walker had been unable to load that much coal, and Mason got the extra cars. He said he preferred to wait and see if he couldn't continue to do that. As for Sproul, the proposed siding was too expensive for him to afford it alone when he was just getting started on three foot coal.

That meant that Sproul's coal would not be mined. The whole problem has wrinkled my brow with worry ever since I came here eight years ago. My station handles so little it cannot show a profit except on coal, and it will close if it doesn't show a profit. Consequently, I managed to coax all the coal business in town to my station only to find I couldn't get the track for it. There is more profit in coal than any other freight, and it would pay the WM to build a siding to handle the business the small coal operators wanted to give them, but there is a rule against that. Coal operators are supposed to build their own sidings. Here, the biggest of them, Mason, started with but two thousand dollars. He made a nice profit during the war, but he is saving it, managing to get along with the room the B&O and WM aren't using on their station sidings. Sproul will be unable to sell his coal, because he has no place to load it. The WM will lose the revenue off of it, and off of two-thirds of Mason's, because the coal operators, not the railroad, are supposed to build the track. The entire situation sounds just exactly like a man.

December 4, 1946

Annie Williams is dead. Fortunately they took her out of her little house on Kentuck a couple of weeks ago. There is a deep snow on the ground now and a hearse would have trouble getting very close to Annie's home. Annie has been dying of cancer for the last year. She insisted on staying in her own home where she lived alone for the last twenty years since the death of her mother. Annie was an old maid, and there were many stories about her.

It seemed the long years of living alone up there on the top of Kentuck where the hills meet the sky, sometimes taunted by passing children, had given her the obsession that everyone was against her. She was always telling anyone who would listen how badly her neighbors treated her, and sometimes her language was very rough. Morally, however, she was a decent woman. One of the jokes was what she told a certain man who came to her house on business and insulted her.

Annie was careless about her appearance ever since I have known her, though she did not have a homely face. She rolled her hair on top of her head and usually part of it would slip away from the pins. She wore disreputable old clothes and tied huge canvas tennis shoes on her feet. She was thin but strong. One warm fall afternoon, I was taking a walk after work. I met her at the foot of the steep path up the mountain, west of the two railroad bridges, taking a short cut to her home on the summit. Over her shoulder she carried a feed sack full of groceries and in the other had a large split basket of house plants. I volunteered to carry the plants and stopped many times on the way to rest. Annie stopped only through courtesy, and of course she had intended carrying both burdens up the hill at the same time.

She explained that Ruby Locke had given her the plants out of her porch boxes because Ruby had all she wanted indoors and these would freeze. Annie said she wanted to keep them through the winter so she could set them out on her mother's grave when spring came. Speaking of flowers reminded her of birds. She said she had always liked to hear the birds sing till the day her mother died, but they made her angry that day. They flitted about the trees singing gaily all day while her mother lay a corpse.

Once, later, when I met Annie in the spring along that woodsy path, my hands full of wild flowers, she invited me up to her place to see her apple trees. She declared they were a fair picture, bent down with white petals. Only once did I ever hear her use the rough language she was noted for, and that was the time we had to sign up for our ration books – which irked more than one of us.

"What was my name?" she railed to me. "I had to tell 'em how old I was, what was the color of my eyes, what was the color of my hair. They asked me everything but the color of my rear end, and all just to get a little bit of sugar."

Down at the Stewart girls' house that night we three, who had gathered around the radio to hear the music, giggled to each other. Only single women could appreciate Annie's feelings.

Annie always kept a couple of big guard dogs on her place whose affection she much cherished, but her most beloved pet was a hog. He had been a runt, and the farmer he belonged to was going to kill him. Annie interceded, planning to raise him by hand and have some pork when fall came. However, she hadn't counted on her heart. When fall came she was so fond of her new pet she couldn't part with him. She wouldn't even put him outside. She had raised him in her kitchen, and she was afraid he'd get cold now that winter was coming. So in her kitchen that big hog stayed for I forget now how many years.

Annie lived on state relief checks. She skimped on her own food to feed her pet and carried big sacks of hog feed up the steep mountain trail to keep him from getting hungry. Her hog became as famous as our falls, and people drove to her place in summer to see him. Finally some state authority made her put the hog in a pen. I never knew whether it was the humane society or the board of health, and whether they did it for Annie's sake or the hog's, but Annie was pretty mad about it.

"That," lectured Esther Collins, the assistant signalman's wife, "is the fruit of living alone."

I ruefully admitted that it was. But I told her I hoped, when I became sixty and people began high-hatting me because I never had a husband, that I could find something to lavish my affection on besides a hog.

Cancer was the cause of the hog's death as well as Annie's. When she first took sick she was sent to the hospital, and the hog was killed, because no one wanted to take care of him. When Annie came home in a few weeks she was inconsolable when she learned what had happened to her pet. It was the beginning of the end. She and her dogs lived together another year while she constantly grew weaker. Relatives offered her a room in their home, but she clung to her own fireside. Finally the neighboring farm women she had so often accused of being her enemies, had to make daily visits to bring her food and tend to her needs. That lasted several months, till her niece took her to town two weeks ago.

Annie made no protest this time about moving. They said she awaited her niece's arrival anxiously, afraid she wouldn't come. You get that way when you are very sick.

December 9, 1946

The coal strike is over till April. It ended as suddenly as it started, and just when things looked worst. The Railroad Center had been a gloomy sight when I went home the Saturday of the last day of November. The lights of all the shop windows were out and so were the colored lights that had been strung across the street for Christmas. Shoppers bought sparingly. Everyone was beginning to feel the pinch. Coal was doled out by the retail dealers a ton at a time to those completely out of coal. Industries closed down one by one as they ran out of fuel. Everyone expected to be out of work by Christmas.

Worst hit of all were the miners themselves. Life isn't worth much to a miner without a big pay before Christmas. A miner's wife, waiting in the streetcar terminal, said to the woman sitting beside her.

"You don't know how it is. Out of work so much, the uncertainty, never having money when you need it or knowing when you are going to have it. It's terrible."

Over in the Scott's Run district near Morgantown, WV, Richard Martin kidded an old pal who is now a family man. " I hear you are striking because of the grueling fifty-four hour week?"

"I haven't worked fifty-four hours a week since the last strike!" the miner snarled with an oath. He explained that the coal car shortage had cut them down to four days a week all summer, after losing six full weeks of work by a strike in the spring.

Yet there was no bitter condemnation of John L. Lewis. They felt they deserved more money, that other trades got more, that their old leader, who had brought them so far, deserved their support, that he must have some good reason for all this, much as they hadn't wanted it on Christmas.

Meantime the strip mines were harvesting fortunes with state police to guard them. They were filling the most extreme needs, but they amounted to only a drop in the bucket when it came to filling the nation's coal order. Mason, on the other hand, barely made expenses. Too many of his men were afraid of the situation and stayed at home. Most of the time he succeeded in loading two cars instead of the three he was geared to load and the third car was his profit. With every industry in the country on the verge of closing for lack of coal, everyone's temper was rising when I locked my office last Saturday, December 7, to go to the Railroad Center for the weekend.

I had to travel to River Junction to get a westbound train home which didn't stop here. As soon as I got on the eastbound train the conductor told me with a big grin that the strike wasn't over. He had reason to grin. If it had continued, his train was to make its final trip the following day. He said he didn't know the details, but the man had called to him at the Railroad Center that it was off till April.

Western Pennsylvania gave a sigh of relief. At River Junction, where I spent two hours in the B&O tower listening through the loud speaker to the dispatcher running trains while I waited for mine, everyone was smiling.

They didn't know any details either. They just knew the strike was over. When I reached the Railroad Center, elation was in the air. Shop windows were blazing with lights and Christmas decorations were all alight. Streets flowed and jammed with automobiles, and crowds pushed and laughed on the sidewalk. In Burn's drugstore a high school girl excitedly began her Christmas shopping by calling between moving heads to her mother to ask the brand of tobacco Uncle John smoked. When her mother told her, she scanned the list offered and called back.

"Well I guess Uncle John will have to change his brand!"

With everybody back to work it looks like this last week of the deer season will be left to the experienced hunters. The first week it was said there were more hunters in the woods than was ever known to be out heretofore. Several men were killed and deer lost their lives on every hill. Beautiful, antlered, tan-colored animals, strapped to autos, with their stiffened legs sticking up grotesquely, were seen going through town most every day. It seemed most of adult Western Pennsylvania was out with buckshot and a high-powered rifle while we who want no part in the gory affair sat back and talked of the danger and the lack of sportsmanship. I felt sorriest for the deer seen dashing through the woods with his leg shot off.

But this week the fever is over. With the miners back in the pits, all the other folks who had been laid off can go back to work, too, and everyone wants to earn some money for Christmas. The newspapers carried big headlines about the return to work. The most significant comment, however, was a photograph carried on the front page of the Pittsburgh Press.

Under the title "These Three Were Not Alone" was a photo of the backs of three miners as they walked to work at Cloverdale, near Pittsburgh. The landscape was the barren one of the mining district. The air was hazy with early morning's smog. The road was a mud one. Up on a cinder back to their right stood a track of those coal hoppers that are so in demand this fall, because hoppers mean work, and, therefore, food, clothes, and shelter for men like them, and luxury for the man who owns the coal. In the distance the high, ugly mine tipple reared through the smog. The men's dark clothes looked almost like prison garb. They wore caps, carried dinner buckets and had lamps strapped to their waists.

They were going back to the eternal darkness of their underground pits, and they carried the rest of us on their backs. If they stayed there, we prospered. If they quit, or anything else happened to halt the income from the black fuel they dug out of the bowels of the earth, we would go bankrupt. These were the men who were asking more financial reimbursement, a welfare fund to take care of their old age, their sicknesses and accidents. These were the men who got criticized when they threw money away at some brightly lit bar, one place at least where they could find light and warmth. These were the kind of men who put three hundred dollar living room suites in a rough frame dwelling, or drove an automobile fit for a millionaire. Did anyone have more right to luxury than those who spent their working hours in a black, grimy hole, forever in danger of getting smashed by falling slats, choked with gas, burned by an explosion, or cut up by a mine car? Even as I gazed at them I knew that I, too, might be criticizing when spring came – if they took our living away from us.

December 23, 1946   Tragedy headlines the news from our town again, highway tragedy. Last week sixteen-year-old Wayne Wable was killed when he jumped from a moving truck. He was a big boy who didn't like school. This fall he quit and got himself a job in the woods cutting mine props. He had caught a ride to work in a truck, but the driver had forgotten where he wanted off. Wayne jumped instead of calling to the driver. An instant's bad judgment dashed away a mother's sixteen years of endeavor, and they say she is heartbroken.

Tonight the hotel waitress rushed into the dining room to tell me someone had just phoned that Clyde Groff and Frank Tissue had been killed in Frank's truck. Frank Tissue was the father of Gene Simpson's wife, the grandfather who had taken in her orphan sons. The waitress said he had sold his blacksmith shop and seemed to have set out to drink up what he had received for it. Mrs. Tissue, in desperation, had "shut the tap off" at the local bar, but being unable to buy liquor there only drove him to River Junction, and he had been killed coming back. The waitress claimed it was always better to let the men drink at their bar so they wouldn't be out on the highway. She said, though, that she was glad she had not sold the men the drinks that had caused their death. She seemed to forget that Clyde and Frank had learned the liquor habit at the bar she served.

Clyde was single, discharged from the army about a year ago. Folks told fondly about the time he was drafted. He had had poor eyesight and little education, and the army examiner complained he didn't read very well.

"Well, hell," Clyde had come back, "I'm not goin' over there to read to 'em!"

The army passed him – all the way to North America and up through Italy. He had some narrow escapes, but he came home with glasses, gray hair, and considerable more knowledge than he had gone away with. However, he was an even worse drunkard. He, too, was supposed to be working in the woods, but he spent more time in the barroom.

Clyde was Goldie Little's brother, and he had made his home with her. I stopped there after supper to express my sympathy and then excused myself to deliver Christmas presents and mail local Christmas cards. During the evening I was told Frank had gotten too drunk to drive and had given the wheel of the truck to Clyde, who couldn't drive well even when sober. The men said Clyde must have died happily, because he was going at a crazy speed when he ran into a wall. I wondered how Mrs. Tissue would get along, with children of her own at home and three grandsons to feed. They replied that mother's assistance for a brood like that would give her a better living than Frank had provided.

December 27, 1946

I finally did celebrate Christmas. For a week before it arrived, I played checkers on the station siding with coal hoppers and boxcars of limestone, trying to keep space for each. The ground was covered with snow and sleet. The conservation office had picked that inopportune time to ship government lime to the farmers. They shipped six carloads all at once, over a thousand paper bags in each car. The head of the trucking company wanted just one car at a time, but when I had the others set off elsewhere I wasn't pleasing my chief, and when I pleased him, my costumers objected. Finally the mines ran entirely out of hoppers, and I filled the station siding with lime and assured the truckers I would fix the reports so they wouldn't have to pay demur-rage.

Unloading proved a slow procedure with a man going ahead of the trucks in a pickup to ash the driveways into farmers' barns. They unloaded the last car as I locked the station door to go home for Christmas Eve.

By nine that evening I had the last silver icicle and light on the Christmas tree in my home in the Railroad Center and was stretched out on the davenport asleep with the radio pealing out Christmas music. My mother and sister woke me at midnight to hear the radio's chimes and carols. The lighted tree seemed to transform the room. The music, too, was beautiful. All at once I realized that this was Christmas, and the angels had come back as they did every year for a few hours to work their miracle on human hearts.

Perhaps next year, I thought, would be a better one. Perhaps men would find some way to come to agreement without strikes. Some means might be found, too, to continue selling what was produced so there would be no depression, and a way arrived at for nations to settle their differences without going to war. Those were the things we feared most. And, perhaps, if enough of us wanted it and prayed for it, there really would be "Peace on Earth."

January 9, 1947   New Year's brought us snow, sleet, and high wind. That week, while other families cleared away the Christmas litter, the Squire did a different kind of cleaning up. There was the fellow who took two Christmas trees off Charlie Locke's Christmas tree farm without paying the full market price. And the tree the boys chopped down just outside Ella Brady's door. The latter was sort of a confused affair at first. The boys had cut the tree to put in the Methodist Church for the Christmas entertainment. The lady in charge of training the children for the entertainment had told them to get a big one, and they cut the first big tree they found, serenely oblivious, as is the way of small boys, of the fact it was in Ella's park a short distance from her kitchen. Ella is a Catholic, and she accused the Methodists of coming on her place and cutting her tree. The Methodists said they did not. The idea! They bought their tree at Bob Locke's. Then the little lady who'd done the training explained that, yes, she had the boys bring in a tree, but it was such a scraggly one she hadn't used it, after all. Ella finally let the matter drop on agreement that the boys would plant six trees to replace the one they cut down. Which will at least make them more careful whose property they confiscate in the future.

This week I attended a housekeeping shower given for Walter McFarland and his English bride. The slender girl says she did not mind leaving England, because she had no close relatives. Walter's aunt, who works for Red Cross in the County Seat, says many foreign brides become very homesick indeed. She told of a little French girl from New Caledonia with two babies who got so homesick for her mother. And of English girls who married into Italian or other foreign families, forced to live with their husband's people who spoke little English and lived in the patch, as the company house of the mining towns are called. Walter's aunt said these girls often told the Red Cross, "It was pictured so differently to me." Or, "My husband never told me anything about his family."

There was music and food at the McFarland's that night, and our English bride received enough small necessities to equip her new apartment which is to be over Ray Wolfe's restaurant in the building owned by her mother-in-law.

January 15, 1947

This is the time of the year when our little town is at its worst. The days are still very short. Dawn comes sometime after seven, and sunset is at five. The hills look dark and lonely through the short day, and the sky hangs close above us with thick, gray clouds. The river is full of brown water that snarls in an incessant undertone. So far this winter we have had no very deep nor pretty snows. The outdoors is just dark and dreary. There is no movie or other entertainment in the evening. The stores close at eight, evicting the last loafer, and the nights are long.

The wind cuts coldly when I cross the river in the dark at six in the evening for supper. I can tell by the number of voices in the barroom that most of the sociably inclined men of the town have gathered there. A younger group of males collect around the table in the hotel dining room to drink beer and play the jukebox. The younger group mostly belong to the 52-20 club. By six they are going strong, for by six the outdoors is something they prefer to forget. Sometimes there is a girl or two at the tables with them.

Tonight I have been thinking about these young men. I don't begrudge them a good time, but I wish it were doing them some good instead of making loafers and drunkards out of them. There is no wholesome entertainment here and what little work there is is of the manual labor type the soldiers had been led to believe they are above. The American Legion talked of establishing a clubroom, but no one was enthusiastic. Whether the legion likes and deserves the reputation or not, a Legion clubroom in this district means only to most folks another barroom, and both the boys and the sober folks think one bar in such a small town is enough.

I would like to see a clubroom that didn't have a bar, but that did have soft drinks, games, a gymnasium, and wholesome reading matter. There should especially be magazines about various trades to arouse the interest of these men who are sinking into lethargy. The same service should provide news of all new work in the vicinity and any openings in the trades in the nearby towns.

January 22, 1947

Yesterday was a day of flying snow and wind with the thermometer going down to zero in the evening. I would not have moved from the glowing coals of my Burnside had it not been a lady was coming from Pittsburgh to organize a PTA. The new principle, a young married man from one of the steel towns, invited all us old maids and bachelors and childless couples as well as the parents to the meeting in hope of getting a group together interested in his school.

Our school is a discouraging problem. Ten years ago the school board attempted to build it of native stones, reasoning they could get the stone free and WPA would donate the labor, enabling them to use their money for structural steel and such materials. But the needed materials were dear and the stone cutting took so long the WPA used up its allotment. The school building has been used in its allotment. The school building has been used in its unfinished state ever since, not plastered, only half wired, and very hard to heat. The State granted eight thousand for completion but state-approved wiring came first, and the lowest bid obtained on that was nine thousand. Therefore the school is still not plastered, still cold, and it was there twenty-seven of us met the lady from Pittsburgh.

Everyone kept their coat on. The lady was cheerful, and we tried to be. She outlined procedure for a PTA, but I doubt if the organization she is sponsoring will be of much value to us. It is too nicey-nice. It does not ask blunt questions and is afraid to campaign for reform. It would be embarrassed if it were ever impolite or got out of its jurisdiction. If we don't do some of those things we are not going to get a better building nor a better school.

The hospitable women of our town served hot coffee and sandwiches after the meeting, and the principle drove the Pittsburgh lady to her bus for a long, cold night ride to her home.

January. 31, 1947

Mrs. Beatty died in the River Junction hospital since my last entry. The Beattys were a quiet, childless, middle-aged couple who lived in a neat white house on Commercial Street. Beatty is a painter and a good man. They came up from Winchester, VA, several years ago and liked the mountains so well they settled here. Beatty will take his wife back to Virginia for burial and will stay a while with her brother. I keep remembering the time he got up in a revival meeting last winter, after recovering from a severe illness, and said he was grateful to God for his life and health. This winter he has to learn to accept bereavement without becoming embittered.

The biggest entertainment of the winter was staged last evening. The high school put on a play, and it was a huge success. The two young lady teachers had labored for weeks with their giggling student actors, but they said the thrill they got when they peeped at the packed auditorium was worth it. That was the best of it to most of us, too. Everyone was there. All the townsfolk together at one time, all the folks from the country that we so seldom get to see. The students had most of their awkwardness trained away from them and really did put on a fair performance. One of our ladies who sings, a local quartette, and that church orchestra that has been on hand for everything this winter, furnished music in intermissions. When it was all over there was laughing and handshaking and neighbors exchanging greetings as the crowd moved slowly out. The financial results were $140 for student activities, with a donation of $25 collected from the audience by our Civic Club for the Infantile Paralysis Drive.

I ate my last dinner at the hotel tonight. Hereafter I will eat it at Ray Wolfe's where I eat my lunch. Food is cheaper at Ray's. He does his own cooking, aided by his wife, whereas the hotel-keeper must hire cooks that are constantly deserting him. This week he is using the woman who usually does hotel chores for free beer.

Beer had a lot to do with my leaving. I was tired of eating beside the stench of it. Tired of coming in evenings to find our discharged soldiers had wasted their day over the oilcloth covered tables on the opposite side of the room. Their sodden faces and bleary eyes that had once been bright and alive are not good appetizers for the evening meal. Worse still was my discovery that the hotel was being used as a meeting place for illicit romances. An innkeeper need only be careless or absent for a little while for the unsavory to take over.

Ray Wolfe's place is makeshift in many ways, but he takes time out to cook me a wholesome meal for which I am grateful. Ray is in his forties and always liked to cook. Being single when the war came along, he joined the Navy, not because he wanted to fight, but because he couldn't sit back and see his nephew, Walter McFarland, and all the other boys who were just kids to him, go out and do the job without offering to help. Actually he is a timid, nervous sort of fellow, but the Navy didn't turn him down. They put him in the Seabees, and the Seabees put him in a galley where he served long and well. When he got out he took over the vacant storeroom in his sister's building, put tables in it and stove behind the counter. The walls and floor are ugly, boys bang pinball machines incessantly while they drink pop and eat ice cream, but no one is drunk – and I'm allergic to drunks.

February 1, 1947

The dreariness of winter was lightened last night for many of us church women when Amy Locke entertained the Ladies Bible Class. Amy is Charlie's wife, our most prosperous merchant. Amy, on the stout side, is always immaculate. Her skin is clear, and her graying hair softly waved. Her home spells luxury to all of us, the big white house on the hill above the store. Her furniture is early American, her long living room complete to grandfather's clock and fireplace. A wood fire burned cheerfully last night, and the cushions on her davenport were so soft that the doctor's daughter said, if she ever let her husband lie down on such a couch, she'd never be able to get him up. There is a conservatory of potted plants. Upstairs are four poster beds, hooked rugs and handmade quilts. But the most luxurious room in Amy's home to the wives of our little town is her kitchen.

It has peach walls and a shiny dark blue floor that never seems to get dirty. There is every electrical device imaginable. Water pours from faucets that don't even splash. To the women who spend their winter days carrying in water from a pump covered with snow, carrying out buckets of waste water, lugging in buckets of coal and carrying out ashes, sweeping and scrubbing grimy floors, Amy's kitchen is a dream. It even has a maid, Betsy.

Betsy is a deaf mute who knows by instinct, a gesture, or the look in your eye what is desired. We church women giggle over the little stories about her. She goes to church with the Lockes, but Amy says, when the Methodists were getting a very poor grade of supply ministers, that Betsy made motions she preferred the Baptist church, their minister was better. So we know a bore can be detected even by the deaf. And when a visiting minister insisted on shouting to the rafters Betsy motioned he hurt her ears.

After our business meeting there were games and prizes and a pink and white lunch reminiscent of Valentine's Day. The dessert course was ice cream topped with out-of-season strawberries. It was midnight before we reluctantly left the luxury of Amy's for the cold dark outside of her home.

February 11, 1947

The groundhog saw his shadow the second day of February, and his prediction has held true. Slashing snow and sleet came over the mountains the following day like a wave bearing down on us. By night the snow was deep and the thermometer nearing zero. The next morning I crawled out of bed early because I was too cold to sleep, but the Squire had preceded me and had the kitchen stove blazing and the tea kettle singing. He admitted that he, too, had slept cold. Said the thermometer was four below.

Scalding tea warmed me a little. The leaden sky was but faintly light when I went on duty at seven. The heavy atmosphere had smoldered out the fire, and the office had the temperature of a refrigerator. Trains were coming. I had to work a half hour – putting up orders to a fast freight, moving a westbound off the passing siding – before I could take time out to build a fire. My fingers were numb with cold. The fires I started in the waiting room and office stoves sputtered reluctantly, but I attacked them with the poker and soon had them roaring angrily. I took the broom outside to sweep paths till the trackmen had time to shovel the snow off the platform. The wind cut like a knife with a cold that had the feel of the Arctic in it.

We were praying for the moonlit nights last summer. The Lord never becomes a too indulgent father. We are too prone to take Him for granted, too quick to think ourselves the lords of the universe who manage everything. It only takes a too hot, or too cold a breath from the Giver of weather to remind us we are human flesh and had best not strut. This month we have been given cold to combat to keep us from growing soft. For ten days we have known nothing but snow and zero temperatures outdoors, and constant work indoors to keep warm and moderately clean. My bedroom is always cold. My office fire always needs attention. I carry out ashes, carry in coal, sweep, dust, and sweep some more. No matter how much I sweep, small particles of coal escape the broom to crush irritatingly under my feet. I was glad to escape it all for a weekend at home in the Railroad Center Saturday where my mother had such delicacies as crisp salads and a warm bathroom. My lame sister and I even braved the storm to see a Bing Crosby movie. I lay in bed that night, warm and clean and comfortable, my ears alert long after my body was ready for sleep. I could hear the trains up the river at the small, weather-beaten office where I used to work at night. A 1200s foghorn whistle was calling his half-frozen flagman. Another train was asking for the operator's signal, and I knew a young fellow was battling the storm in and out of his office, throwing switches, putting up orders, trying to fire his stove and listen to the dispatcher at the same time. The wind still beat at the panes, and the trains were still talking when I drifted off into slumber.

The houseplants I had in my office windows were frozen when I went to work Monday morning. Even the ink was frozen. But this afternoon the sky cleared and the sun came out. My bedroom seemed warmer when I went up to dress for supper. I rolled up the shades and saw the red disk of the sun sinking behind a lattice of tree trunks on the top of the hill. It was after five o'clock. The days were growing longer, and my spirits lifted at the realization. The rose-colored sky the sun left was frigid, but there would be more light from now on. It is the dark of January that is depressing.

February 12, 1947   Old Jim Zebley burned to death last night. Jim was eighty-seven years old and had the reputation of being the dirtiest man in the district, speaking from a hygienic standpoint. It is said he once lived a whole winter in a shelter made out of mine props. He was sent to the County Home once, but he ran away, preferring to fend for himself. Lately he has been living in a shack near Mason's mine.

The miners often gave him a helping hand. One of them gave him a good mattress, but he sold it because he wanted the money worse. He lived on an old age pension and could have lived better, but, from what the men told, it seemed he very seldom washed either himself, his clothes, or his cooking utensils. We women didn't know much about him except that the men shook their heads after a visit to his shack. They said he could stand more self-imposed hardship than any man in the county. He would have been living still if he hadn't gone to sleep while he was smoking in bed.

When the red light of the fire was first seen against the sky at Robinson's service station they thought it was the mine or the stable of ponies. Mason raced to the mine and found Jim's shack on fire, Jim still on his burning mattress suffocated by smoke.

There will be a service for Jim in the Baptist Church tomorrow, and he will be buried in a country graveyard beside his mother. Mason says the old fellow had made that request of him just a few weeks ago.

February 19, 1947   The WM has finally received the fifteen new engines they have been expecting for the last six months, and now that they have them they don't seem to be sure what they are going to do with them. They look to us as though they were made for level country. They have been tried out between Cumberland and Baltimore, and the officials brought one over here Sunday. It was the 1401. I caught my first glimpse of it shortly after I opened the station Monday as it went by with the Reading Hot Shot. I wasn't impressed. It is a coal-burning locomotive, but it isn't as big as our 1200s or as dramatic. It didn't even seem to be going as fast.

Our 1200s are really an engine. To be more exact, they are a mallet type of locomotive and are two engines in one. They are 118 feet long and have two sets of three drivers on each side, two sand domes and even two smoke stacks. Their whistle is a foghorn, and their big headlight is set low. Their boiler is on a pivot so that coming around a curve it juts off at an angle instead of riding rigidly above the wheels. Timid ones, unfamiliar with my favorite locomotive, seeing it cut a caper like that coming at them full speed, are sure it is going to jump the track. Then the engineer goes by laughing. They can race right up the mountain with three thousand tons hung on behind them and can go forty-five miles an hour if they are not weighted down with too large a train.

As the PRR has been reminded again by the wreck on their Horseshoes Curve, the question is not how fast a locomotive can travel but what speed the track is good for. The WM's engineering department has limited speed to thirty-five miles an hour. The new engines have high driving wheels like a passenger locomotive for more speed, but more speed is not needed on this division. They have only four drivers on each side, which makes them a smaller engine with less power than either our 1200s or 1100s. The 1401 hung up this morning on the grade at Fort Hill with only 2800 tons. The aim of the railroads for many years has been longer trains and not so many of them. Therefore, it looks as though the 1400s traveling will be confined to the flat land of Maryland where they can haul a longer train.

Anyway, I have changed my pronoun for them. I am going to call them what passenger train engineers call their locomotives – She. Our old 1100s that roar up the steepest grade in the mountains with 4200 tons are a huge, lumbering male. Our 1200s are a lithe, strong, sport of a fellow, fast as the red wings painted on WM tenders. But these small, speedy, unpredictable weaklings will never be thought of as belonging to any but the feminine gender.

February 25, 1947

Those pretty snows we didn't have in January have been with us most of the month. The zero temperatures of the first part of the month moderated just enough for good snowing, then the mercury went down again. We have grown used to a white landscape. The river is low and clear now, a dark, satiny streak upon the snow. The falls are a mint cocktail, bubbling as it pours into the dark pool circled by white. An etching of almost black leaves of the rhododendron can be seen on snow-topped rocks along Meadow Run, whose still waters are all but covered with snow. And always the pines stand up, black silhouettes against bare, interlacing branches.

Jud Orndorff's track gang is split in two shifts, one group working all night to keep switches free of snow. I leave my station unlocked so they can come in to warm. Highway gangs work all night, too, and pound Ray out of bed at 5 a.m. for food. Rural school children crowd into his place at noon for warm lunches. Meals are all I have to break my own monotonous round of desk work, firing stoves and cleaning up the dirt they make. The stirring, shaking, and shoveling to keep my stove hot leaves a settlement of black dust on every desk and paper, and by the time I have it cleaned off them I find it has all accumulated on me. Only evenings are pleasant when I loaf in front of that glowing fire, that took so much work all day, reading the newspapers, listening to the radio, sometimes dozing. But my bed is always cold, and I pile everything available on it before I raise the window an inch and retire. On top of the other covers goes my old tweed work coat, which I thought disgustingly the other night, as I crawled under it, smelled something like a wet cat. I didn't think about it long, however. That tweed coat is warm, and I was sleepy.

February 26, 1947

I peeped out the bathroom window this morning through a blustery snowstorm and saw that Mason and Walker's coal hadn't been moved. Unless it was moved the miners would be unable to work, because there was no room to push empty hoppers in the place of the loads. I hurried a little faster into my clothes. Bad weather had made traveling hard to and from the mines for those on side roads, and some miners had lost several days work already. I hated to see them lose another.

When I got to the kitchen I found the Squire had troubles of his own. The furnace's water pipes were leaking, he said. If the leak got worse the fire would have to be taken out and the furnace torn down. We both fervently hoped that would happen in better weather than the present.

The fire was out in the office stove. The dispatcher said the coal would not be moved. An eastbound freight train had wrecked up the line at midnight and blocked all traffic.

By eight o'clock my office was warm. I sat at my desk listening to officials – engineer of maintenance, division engineer, supervisor of track, train-master, and master mechanic – berating the weather. They called from a phone box at the wreck to the clerks coming to work in their Baltimore and Cumberland offices and had them fill out reports of the derailment. Fourteen cars of coal, pipe, and brick were off the track, eleven of them over the hill, four of that amount in the river. There were two feet of snow and a blizzard raging. Three thousand dollars damage to the track, $4,500 to equipment. They didn't estimate the damage to the spilled lading. That would be a job for the gentlemen who would come out from the freight claim agent's office in Baltimore. It would have been a worse job if it had been the train ahead of this one that had wrecked. That had been mostly meat, butter, and eggs from the Chicago packing houses. The officials said the wreck was caused by a broken rail.

In other words, winter was laughing at them. They employ track-walkers for the particular purpose of finding broken rails. They pay four hundred dollars a day for the test car of the Sperry Rail Service to go over their railroad once a year to find the flaws in the rails the track-walkers can't see. This device is smarter than a man. It finds every weak spot in the steel that is liable to break and marks it with white paint. After it passes foreman change every unsafe rail. There also are automatic electric signals, charged from wells of batteries sunk in the ground, which are wired to the rails and from one rail to another. These are supposed to fall to a stop indication of either a switch is open or a rail is broken. Winter got around it all.

Winter made the rails brittle so they would break away. It made the nights cold, so one broke under a train in the dark of the night. But it didn't break in two, just the head cracked when the meat train went by. The electric current kept going through, keeping the signal clear. Then another train sped up the mountain. The head popped out, and eleven cars tumbled down the snowy bank.

I listened to the terminal yardmasters reporting. The WM yards at the Railroad Center were full of loads because nothing had been moved out of it since the wreck. The PLE terminal seven miles west, where the freight comes in from Pittsburgh, reported three hundred coal on hand, another hundred coal and a hundred fast freight to arrive soon. Most of the coal was for the Port Covington Piers at Baltimore for export. Europe was having a cold wave, too. This coal would be moving slowly even when the track was clear, because Port Covington was having troubles of its own, especially with strip coal that is always wet and quick to freeze. It reported most coal frozen in the cars. The big cranes that pick up a hopper and dump its contents in the hold of a ship, or on a barge for coastline movement, were having trouble dumping a hundred cars a day compared to their usual eight hundred.

The one question yardmasters wanted to know was how soon trains would be moving. How soon could they move something out of their yards so they could take more trains into it? The Train-master said 1 p.m. He was making no attempt to pick up the wrecked cars. The wreck and track crews were merely throwing them out of the way and rebuilding the track. Cars and lading could be picked up some other day. The important thing was to get back in the business of transportation.

I think that is what I love about a railroad. It never cries over an accident. In the years I have sat at a WM desk I have heard all sorts of catastrophe, traffic slowed to a trickle by winter, heartbreaking wrecks, more heartbreaking floods, but as the reports went in I have scarcely ever even heard an exclamation. There was just that toneless and inevitable question: How soon can we get a track through?

Jud's motor car had been thrown hurriedly onto the track at seven this morning and, with heads bent low against the freezing wind, he had sped his gang the 25 miles up the river to the wreck. Johnny Hiles, graying, slow of step, was left to keep the switches clean. He made the two-mile round trip between the east and west end passing siding to the west after he had eaten his lunch and bought himself a paper of tobacco. He said he chewed a powerful lot of tobacco when he was alone.

He returned slowly through the snow, close to exhaustion, as I was closing the station at four. The rest of the gang was still at the wreck. But the track was open, and trains were moving out of the terminals as quickly as they could be called. Wading toward the Squire's, I thought there is at least one nice thing about February. It's a short month.

March 4, 1947

At first March didn't seem any different, just more snow and cold. But there was a difference. The wind was stronger, and the snow came in flurries instead of the steady fall of snowflakes. Last night was very stormy. Track-men swept switches all night, the main highway was drifted to one-way traffic, and the side roads are blocked. Mason's men have not been able to get to work for two days.

Nevertheless, the WM has licked its traffic congestion. The new engines were returned to Maryland, and the chief is using his dependable old goats for extra power. These are the WM's small 800s that have hauled the West Virginia traffic up a steep, sharply-curved roadbed for 45 years. They serve as helpers and local freight engines on this division. Sometimes he double heads two 800s with 5,000 tons. The operators call them "a pair of jeeps." Sometimes he uses an 800 and a 1200 and hauls even more. Today, trains were moving out of the terminals a few hours after they came in.

Trainmen have been overworked to accomplish this, and it is not unusual to see a fireman go by nodding and a flagman fast asleep. Their eight hours rest in home terminals means from the time they cut off at the yard office until they report to it again, or less than five hours in bed. Yesterday a blazing hot box went by, but when I held my fingers to my nose to tell the flagman that he had one stinking, he was too list in slumber to see. We operators arranged between us to stop him at the next office.

Wreck cranes from both terminals came out yesterday to re-track the cars derailed last week. Their efforts to lift heavy loads of brick and pipe up the steep bank were without success. Today they began transferring the lading into other cars. Several thousand bricks had to be relayed up the bank from one man to another, and the car it was being loaded in had to be moved in the clear whenever a train came. At the end of the day the Supervisor said he had 2,000 brick loaded, that it would take two more days to finish the brick, and then he would start on the pipe. A crane can be used to lift a few pieces of that at a time. Some work train next summer will probably scoop up the coal with a clam shell.

While this was being done, the Superintendent called all of us agents to inquire where the sun came up at each station and what hour would be best for taking a photograph of track and landscape. He said he wanted a nice snow scene for the President of the WM, who uses them for advertising and Christmas cards. I managed to resist wisecracking that the sun came up in the east and how about an artistic slant across the wreck, and dutifully explained the sun came up behind my signals, and the best scene could be caught in the morning. A photographer started over the road the next morning in one of the official automobiles, which are equipped with flanged wheels that run on the track. He got caught in snow squalls as soon as he started and turned back after snapping a couple of scenes up the line. The operator says, if he had equipment to take pictures in a snowstorm, they should be beauties.

The quarries the conservation office has contracted with to supply the farmers with limestone sent out another car last night, giving them a perfect score. Every time the farmyards have been blocked with snow this winter they send out a car of ground limestone. But, with boxcars so scarce to ship it in, the farmers tell me they will take it anytime, and that the highway crews have promised the secondary roads will be open tomorrow. I believe they will be. The wind blew the clouds out of the sky this afternoon, and the sun came out over the blustery snow to alleviate the chill cut of the gales.

March 11, 1947

The sun has been shining between little skiffs of new snow for the last week, turning the sunny spots to mud and taking an inch each day off snowdrifts. The Squire said the drifts were still high as a man on Sugar Loaf when he went up yesterday for the first time in a month to see how his tenant farmer was taking care of his stock. A fifty dollar calf had been choked to death, he said, because they hadn't nailed a board back that had been kicked off a stall.

Hensel Daniels came in today for the statement of his earnings last year to use in making out his income tax return. Hensel can't read, but he knows the necessary papers he has to have. Someone else will make out the statement for him, and he will sign with his X. Hensel, like Johnny Hiles, is a bachelor member of the track gang. He is a member, that is, when the weather is good. When the snow gets too deep for walking from his pioneer home on Maple Summit, where he supports his mother, sister, and a couple of stray nephews, Hensel arranges to get himself furloughed and draws his unemployment insurance. "Rocking chair money" he calls it. He said today he had been doing some trapping, too, and shot a couple gray foxes. The fox furs brought him three dollars apiece and an extra five dollars per fox, bounty from the State. Hensel thanked me politely in his mountaineer accent for his statement, charged me to take care of myself, and invited me up to see his folks.

Johnny Hiles, unlike Hensel, has a fair education and is widely known for his wit. He was in World War I, and I have heard him tell of the days he wandered without food as a messenger to the front. And of the time he rounded a barn to come face to face with a German, which startled each of them so much they ran in opposite directions. Johnny says there are more dogs and more old bachelors in our town than any town of its size he's ever been in. I'd never thought of it before, but when we got to counting them, we decided there were about as many bachelors as there were old maids. I guess we're just not sociable. Johnny says he gets a catalog from a mail order house where a fellow can send and get himself a gun, a hunting dog, or a woman. Johnny has none of the three. He just boards with a relative. He used to live up on Greenbrier beyond the Kentuck school Isabel Wolfe teaches. An old man up there by the name of Hughes had "No Trespassing" signs all over his land and was so radical about it he didn't even like to see people going by on the road. When he died, Johnny declared with finality, "Well, no one else will have it posted."

Isabel tells of a woman who lives on Greenbrier who went on having children after her husband died, supporting them with the money she received from Direct Relief. The Relief department finally sent an investigator. "Do you mean to tell me," the man asked her, "that your husband has been dead ten years, and you have all these young children?"

"Why, hell, man," she came back, "he was the one who died. I didn't."

Isabel likes better to tell of the unpopular preacher the Baptists once had who preached a long sermon on "There is No Hell." She says the next week he got mad at a fellow and told him to go there.

Mr. Martin says that most of the B&O section gang during the war were illiterate, men and boys from hill farms who had never bothered to go to school. Most of them were laid off when the gang was cut last spring during the six-week coal strike and never re-hired. The B&O agent was handed the task of signing up everybody who wasn't working for their unemployment insurance. Mr. Martin says he has to watch and put his finger on the line they are to make their X on each time or "demand if they won't get it over in the exception column. I walked quietly into his waiting room one day when he was signing up such a group and heard a young fellow tell him that he couldn't write his real names. He could only write his nickname.

"Why in the hell," the exasperated little agent demanded, didn't you learn to write your real name instead of your nickname?" I giggled silently.

He told me later I should have been there the time he was making papers out for a fellow who said he was 40 years old but didn't know what year he was born in. The agent wanted to know how he knew he was 40 years old. The fellow replied that he was born the year they planted potatoes at the old log barn. They only planted them there every 10 years. And they have planted them there three times since then.

Amy Locke's story is a little sad. She says a young fellow whose folks always dealt at her store came down from Sugar Loaf a few years ago during the Christmas rush, gazed admiringly at the store's bright decorations, and said,

"I see you're havin' Christmas down here."

Amy agreed they were.

"Don't know," he said, "whether they're gonna have Christmas on Sugar Loaf or not. Didn't hear anything about it. When are you havin' your Christmas down here?"

Amy told him it always came on the 25th of December. Then she asked him if he knew what Christmas celebrated.

She said the boy shifted uneasily. "Why – er – It's some general's birthday or som'p'n, ain't it?"

Amy tried to tell him briefly something of the Christmas story. "Didn't you ever go to Sunday School?" she asked.

"Yes," he told her, "I used to go to Meadow Run sometimes. But I couldn't read, and Miss L---, she taught us, and I didn't pay much attention."

Amy insisted that he ought to go to Sunday School again, that grown folks go to Sunday School, too. And he promised he would. Maybe he'd go up to the new church at Oak Grove.

March 17, 1947

The ice went out of the river last Thursday, March 13, and the stream has been full of muddy water ever since. But the rain that raised the river was brief. The mud froze, and snow flurries followed. Today the ground is white again, and the wind is very cold. It has been blowing the flakes up the river so fast it makes one dizzy to watch. The air is full of swiftly moving white polka dots.

Almost everyone in town has a cold. Even I had one, but it soon left me. Half the miners are sick. The Baptist minister has scheduled a two-week revival service but has been getting sparse congregations.

March 19, 1947

I am trying to collect the data to publish an honor roll in book form of the soldiers from this district. I need their final rank, length of service, the outfit they were in, the battles, medals received, their photograph. The task was handed me by the Baptists who wanted it as a final copy of their church papers, which we circulated to the soldiers during the war and which will now go out of print. Some information I have, but I have found it almost impossible to collect what I do not. Our discharged soldiers want nothing to do with the project. Civilians look puzzled and ask why. I can only guess, but from what little they have told me, I think I can understand.

They are tired, reticent, and fed up with the glory story. They want no spread eagle gushing by home-folks who don't know what they are talking about. To the ex-GI, the Army uniform represents hard, bitter, sometimes nerve-shattering services that are best forgotten. Medals and rank remind them, too, of strutting officers, and they are too American to ever like unquestioning discipline. An American questions everything. Many G.I.'s have become calloused or bitter or carousing and at odds with the idealists and the Church whom they think of as praters of fairy tales. Few are proud of their Army service, because too many had to do things that weren't sporting. They had no desire to kill their fellowmen, or be wounded or killed by them, and they're sort of suspicious of the rest of us, wondering if we didn't get them into the thing in the first place. Certainly they want no photograph of theirs paraded nor published anywhere. And I know that and dread to intrude. Yet, for the sake of the boys who died to stop the evil designs of men, I persevere. Twenty years from now these boys will be forgotten, along with the wounded, the heroic, the suffering. And I'd like to keep some record of them.

Last evening I made four calls before supper. At the first I got some information on a young Marine who had left home for work. A boy was foolish to stay here, his grandfather said. No work, no hope in this town. No wonder the returned soldiers got into devilment. The next two homes housed the families of men who made their living in Mason's mine. They lived in rented houses as bare and battered as some ancient barracks and overflowing with children. Everyone had colds. In the one home, too, there was a small girl just out of the hospital. The mother promised to get the information I wanted from the former soldier who visited them on weekends, a strange fellow with a stutter who had been in North Africa. She sat nursing her infant son who was close to croup while the family milled about her. She looked over her brood and said she hoped to get to at least one church service before the revival ended.

In the other home the 11 Williams lived in two downstairs rooms and two upstairs bedrooms. Little boys were taking freshly washed but stiffly frozen clothes off lines strung across the garden. The mother's eyes were red with the cold she suffered from, and both her baby and her daughters were sick. Jim Williams rested barefoot on a spring-less couch. He said his hands were so cramped after a day's mining he couldn't write the information I needed about his hero son who fell in Normandy. But he'd have his daughters write it. He pulled worn snapshots of Jimmy from his pocket and of the Germans Jimmy had captured.

At the fourth house a GI had bought his young wife a home as bright and pretty as their romance. He had enough of a nest egg left, too, to put himself in the lumber business with which he was familiar. But he would carry shrapnel in his lungs for the rest of his life, and his wife said she was a stranger in our town, and the winter had been lonely despite her happiness. She told me about the young couple who lived in her upstairs rooms, reached by perilously steep outside steps. The husband was a permanently injured veteran of the Navy, something wrong with his back and nerves. I knew from the date I had that he had been on a boat that had been sunk leading the D-Day invasion, that there were months in a hospital, that he had been rescued from another sinking ship in the Pacific. That was more than his landlords knew about him. They said the boy never talked, just went by with his head down. They said he was working in the woods, but to make a living at that he had to work longer hours than he was able. His wife was another of last year's graduates, expecting a child, just home from a hospital treatment.

I used the excuse of supper to keep from visiting them. I didn't know how to ask for the service record of a man who wanted to forget it. I was afraid it would open the flood gates of all their troubles. When I went to the revival after supper the minister complained that so few townsfolk were coming to his meetings. I wondered if it ever occurred to him to go to the townsfolk. They certainly needed a man of God worse than they needed a railroad agent.

March 22, 1947

The first day of spring left us an inch of snow, and snow has been falling all morning. The radio promises better weather for Sunday. And it brought us the welcome news that there would be no mine strike on April Fools Day. The mines' wives, and all of those wives whose living depends on the miners, are to get a break. They will be able to get their new spring outfit this year, and the new house furnishings they will need when housecleaning time comes.

March 24, 1947

The two weeks of revival meetings in the Baptist Church closed last evening without a single new convert, or even an old one going up to the altar to renew his faith. The minister and his soloist was Frank Stewart, nephew of my friends Della and Edith Stewart. He is a big man with prematurely gray hair, a sincere face, and a golden voice that soars up and up without any apparent effort. He has been offered contracts to sing on the radio but says he wants to sing only for the Lord. Therefore he is never heard except at a church service, a funeral, or a wedding. He particularly likes to sing at revival services and has trained his children in music so they can help him. His oldest daughter accompanies him and helps him sing duets. Frank works in a steel mill and drives 50 miles every evening to lead the revival music.

Even Frank's stirring voice and unwavering faith in the Lord, which he poured out on his audiences in song and testimony, brought no noticeable response. The minister accused the town of being too much interested in worldly things to bother about their souls, and that is true. Due to the bungling of adults, who had scheduled everything from a dance to Grange meetings for the Lenten season, no young person has had the opportunity to give much thought to the spiritual side of life. Nevertheless, that is not the whole trouble. The Methodists joined the Baptists Sunday night for the final service, and the church was filled. Frank never sang more entreatingly. Before and after the preacher's sermon, he talked simply and with dignity to the folks he had grown up with, telling them of their need of the Christ. No one moved. No one even raised a hand for a prayer.

I glanced around at the congregation and saw that, for the most part, they were old folks. The pews were filled with the old regulars and those others who are far from regular but who at one time or another had ties with some Protestant church. There were but a couple of ex-G. I.'s present and only a sprinkling of teenagers. Those who most needed Frank's message were not there.

I kept wishing they had been present, even though the pastor's sermon was cold with criticism when it should have been warm with sympathy, and the singer who had found the Way of Life could not make his directions clear to others. I wished that our young people had not only been present, but, if they did not agree with the minister and his soloist, that they had stood up in a body and talked back to them. It would have cleared the air. It would have shocked these spiritual leaders, of course, but it might have opened their eyes, too.

Our young people were not there. They had left church to the old folks. They had come a long way the past few years. High school, army, or war plant were experiences to sharpen but not necessarily to elevate the native intelligence of our boys and girls. Those that clung to the hills now know what the cities are like. In fact, some of our boys know what most of the surface of the earth is like. And their sparse comment has been that the rest of the nations can have it. They feel the same about religion. They no longer feel at home in church. They were with their mates last night, or their sweethearts, or in cliques drinking in some roadhouse brazen enough to serve them on Sunday. But I felt they were uneasy. They had known there was to be a big church meeting, and their gestures of staying away had been made defiantly out of the bitterness in their hearts. Nevertheless, they were present in spirit, and I could hear them talking, something like this:

"Sure, we believe in God just as much as you do. This world didn't just happen. And we have prayed, when we were in need, or scared. But we do our praying in private. We're not in the habit of displaying our deepest emotions in public. This revival you put on every year looks to us like a show for the curious, and we want no part in anything like that.

"We don't trust this altar business anyhow. There always have been altars. They used to be heathen gods. Then the Jews discovered there was but one God, but they worshiped Him just about the same as the heathens did. They used the same old altar and brought their best cattle and sheep and roasted them on it as though they thought the God who created the world was hungry.

"And you're still talking about an altar, though you got the thing twisted around a little different now. You say the story about Adam and Eve really happened instead of being a fable to illustrate an age-old truth. You say that this life is a vale of tears, and no man could have gone to a happier land if Jesus had not come down from Heaven and been killed on an altar in the form of a cross. You say He had to do this to fulfill the law that forbids mankind from going to Heaven, because his ancestors, Adam and Eve and Cain, had sinned and brought a curse upon their offspring. You say that Jesus' death took the curse away, and now all we have to do is go up to your altar, and we'll have Eternal Life. You say we'll be saved then and that we will never sin again.

"Well, we don't believe you. Your whole involved theory sounds to us like the incantations of some more heathen rites. We stay away from your church and refuse to come up to your altar, not because we don't want to live better lives and would like to have a better world, but because your religion sounds a hundred years behind the times, and your sermons make no more sense than a powwow doctor's.

"What do we believe? Well, we believe that Jesus was sent to this world to show folks how to live and get the most out of this life the Lord God gave us. He said there was another Life, so there must be, though it might be quite different from what you think. All the experiences of this world, all the growth that souls make when they lead noble lives, or just try to lead them, surely can't be lost. But that, and what Jesus said, is all we know about the Hereafter. We don't worry about what we don't know, though. We don't think our minds are supposed to be big enough to understand God. And we don't think yours is, either.

One of the things we don't like about your religion is that you hold Eternal Life out to us like a stick of candy. If we come up to your altar, we can have it, otherwise, we can't. You make it sound like a reward you preachers hand out for new members. And you seem to think living according to the rules of the Good Book will follow automatically after we've made this particular trip up your church aisle. Why, you don't even emphasize that we should treat our fellowmen right and take care of our own bodies, because that is the sane and decent thing to do, and we should consider the rights of our brothers. Your story is that we have to do that, because we have to look out for ourselves and get this Eternal Life, which we get by renouncing the life we now have.

"That attitude is anything but inspiring, and it doesn't make any more sense than the rest of your theory. We don't think the Lord wants us to renounce the life, love, and happiness of this world if it is lived decently. And we don't want a reward, anyhow. If we ever do come up to that altar of yours, it will be because we want to get closer to God now and live a better, more spiritual life. We will leave the managing of the Beyond to God who made us.

"Nor do we believe our desire to sin will be magically taken away the minute we come back from your altar. We believe that every day of our life is a struggle between good and evil, the best that is in us, and the worst. If you think you can transform us all in just two weeks and you'll be free to sit around for the rest of the year, you're not fooling anybody but yourself. You get paid for working at least six days a week the same as everybody else, and your job is to find the Truth and bring it to us.

"You have said we prefer to live as we do, and there is nothing you can do about it. Our answer is that we don't prefer it, except when we get discouraged and cynical. We prefer to have a good time and enjoy life, yes. But we want to do better than we have done, and sometimes we try. Unfortunately, between the struggle in our own natures and the lures that are placed in our path by the evil and the mercenary, we have a hard time accomplishing anything. Everywhere we turn, liquor and sex are stuck under our noses. They are in the places we loaf, they are brought to us by our associates, the radio, the magazines, the movies. We are besieged by glitter and lies.

"But when we turn to you preachers, your doctrine seems false, too. And a lot of you don't seem to have as much kindness and understanding in your heart as some army sergeants had. Where's all this love of Jesus you talk about? If you just had that, if you reached out your arms in warmth and welcome, a lot of us would come up to your altar because we need help. But it would be pretty hard, after we've joined the church and shook hands with all the good people, to have them turn cold the next day because we asked for a job and couldn't come up to all the red-tape requirements. Or to be told we are going to have to go out again and nobly sacrifice our lives for our country.

"One little church couldn't do much about jobs and wars, but we feel you could read the Gospel of Jesus more, till His love sunk into your hearts and the circle of His influence moved outward. We'd like to have a saner world to bring our children up in – if there is any hope of a future for them instead of another worldwide conflagration. We came to your church once. But your sermons were dull and included no program for the world we live in and fought hard to save. Your congregation was listless and didn't seem enthusiastic about practicing what they professed to believe. You're mistaken when you say no one cares about the Lord. The fields are white with the harvest. But you got to know how to reap it."

However, if they really had spoken these words, I would have had to have gotten up and answered them. And this is what I would have said:

"You're right as far as you go, but you don't go far enough. You question the beliefs of this minister because you are young. Man always begins by questioning God and ends up when he is old by trusting him. You have heard other, more modern doctrines than this small-town preacher's, and you didn't like them, either, did you? Remember the day in the army camp or the war plant when you were so scared, and you stopped in at the big city church? You came out vaguely dissatisfied, didn't you? You said at the time that it was too big and impersonal, and you didn't know anybody, and you wished you could stop in at a prayer meeting in the little church in your own hometown.

"But you never do stop now that you are here. If you had, you might understand better. The city churches have become too modern for revivals, but the religion of Jesus is evangelical, and His charge was to take it to all the world. When we cease to do that, we have a diluted religion. If you want His doctrines presented in a better way, help us with the presentation. This nation will be just as good or just as bad as you, who are younger than we, eventually make it. If you want the Lord's work done, you'll have to do it. You say your hands are not clean enough to bring the Living Bread? Neither are mine. Perhaps the preacher's aren't. But the Lord's work is going to have to be done by us. There will be no saints coming down from Heaven to do it for us. We have got to somehow wash our hands and take the Bread of Life to those who are younger than we are, and work with the preachers we have, not the great leaders we had hoped for."

And then an old voice would have interrupted me, the spokesman for the white-haired bishops and elders of the Methodists and Baptists who sit at the conference table and send out the ministers to their districts. And he would have said this:

"We send you the best preachers we have. Some are better than you deserve and others, we grant you, are poor makeshifts, indeed. But we can only send you the material you send us, and for many years the material has been second-rate, the misfit, the dreamer, never the valiant leaders we need. The men of leadership are in industry. They are doing everything from practicing law to flying B-29s, from heading industrial corporations to studying engineering. The ministry is the most despised trade in America. If you can't do anything but be a preacher, your friends think you don't amount to much. No boy wants a trade that does not give him the respect of his fellows and pay him a living wage. This thing has become a vicious circle. You don't respect the minister, and, therefore, we can't find ministers to train that you can respect. We want prophets to cry out against the sins of the world. We need dominant young leaders who can rally the people. And we believe the Lord will send them – in time. But if you want them in time to save our world from another catastrophe, you had better begin considering the preacher an important man in your community and teach your children to respect the Church."

March 25, 1947   We are having another March blizzard. Wind and snow are sweeping up the river, breaking branches off the treetops, shaking the semaphore pole, and beating on the window panes of Adeline Locke's home where her mother, Claire Porter, has come home to lie a corpse. Claire is lying in the dining room that Adeline has just finished remodeling. Adeline had a carpenter working for months taking the back porch in with the dining room and enclosing it in glass so they could lounge there and look out on the lawn, the river, Ferncliff and the mountain beyond. Red velvet drapes are hung over the glass now, and Claire lies there in state, clad in a pale blue dress, her gray hair softly waved, and her smooth face belying her 70 years. Schoolboy Kenny Wolfe, awed by the passing of one of our best families, confided to me that she was the most beautiful corpse he had ever seen. That was easy to understand. Claire had had a nice winter visiting. She was at peace when flu suddenly complicated her asthma, and she had slept her last day away and gone to meet Dalton.

Dalton Porter was the kind of man that decent women think of with a lump in their throat, a pang of regret that his kind seems to be dying out. He was a cultured, courteous gentleman of the old school who could not understand why the younger generation was not taught music and good manners as carefully as his had been. If Dalton Porter ever used an oath it must have been very quietly. He never swaggered, lied, nor cheated. He started business up on Meadow Run, where he had a gristmill back in the 90s. The location is still called Porter's Mill. When he moved his mill into town, he was grinding his own feed and wanted a larger market, but of late years he had confined his business to selling balanced, vitamin-reinforced stock feed to the farmers. He always bought his feed in carload lots from a modern plant in Ohio and was my station's best customer.

When Dalton was stricken with paralysis, Claire took over the mill and ran it for several years. I liked the clean fragrance of the sacked grain when I would stop in for a business visit. There was stock feed, horse feed, pig feed, calf starter, laying mash, and even dog feed, piled in high rows on the white board floor. Healthy cats guarded it from rats. Claire would brush a couple of them off a chair in her miniature, paper-cluttered office, and we'd sit and talk till both of us realized we were going to be late for supper. Claire always had an extra dollar for anything townsfolk or school children were selling and usually gave them a double order. Christmas, anniversaries, and wedding showers were not complete without her check that would buy a much larger present than the recipient had ever dreamed.

Then Dalton died, and Claire took to her bed. Finally she sold the feed business to Adeline's father-in-law, Charlie Locke. Last fall she recuperated enough to go on a visit that lasted the rest of her life. She went to New York and visited her eldest granddaughter who lived in a tiny apartment, which was a novelty to Claire. Then she visited her eldest daughter in a comfortable home near Pittsburgh. There she stayed all winter gaining weight and rest from the change. She wrote me of the places she had gone, the shows she had seen, all of it a lark after so many years at home. She liked the decent stories of the movies, but when she was driven into Pittsburgh to see the stage presentation of 'The Voice of the Turtle,' she was scandalized and wrote me her disapproval.

However, the calendar was pointing toward spring, and she could no more stand a summer away from our little town than Dalton could have stood it. On summer evenings one could always see Dalton leave his white house under the spreading trees and walk down past Castle Rock to Meadow Run bridge, drinking in the beauty of the sunset above the high peak and its reflected glory on the water at the bend of the river.

"It's a scene I never tire of," he once told me.

Nor have I. Nor had Claire Porter. She went shopping her last trip in Pittsburgh, bought her Easter hat and some household gadgets she'd be needing when she got back to doing her housework. She arranged to come home this last Sunday. And she did.

But not the way she had planned.

March 29, 1947

When we arose yesterday morning, we found the air clear and very cold, and the thermometer five above zero. Then a big red disk of sun came up behind my signals and blinded me with its brilliance as I worked at my desk, and I knew winter was over. By noon the earth was warm and so was my bedroom – till next winter rolls around. The sky grew cloudy as though thinking of rain. It was still cloudy when a group of us women met at the home of 81-year-old Mrs. Alice Locke for the monthly social meeting of the Ladies Bible Class.

Mrs. Alice Locke is the teacher of the class, though she usually leaves that task to her assistants these days. Last night, however, she was bent on doing a few things for us personally. She had crocheted each one of us a pincushion in the form of a hat and tied baby ribbon around it. She recited her favorite poem. She sat smiling while we entertained ourselves by buying foolish copies of Easter bonnets we had brought each other, which we wore while refreshments were served. The purchase money went to swell our flower fund. When Mrs. Locke's daughter, Mrs. Gwen Waters, had carried the last plates back to the kitchen, and the group around the piano quit singing to hunt their wraps, Mrs. Locke was still the gracious hostess bidding us goodnight.

April 5, 1947   The very first day of April seemed spring-like. Hard as it was to believe after such cold, I could see a faint, greenish cast on the hillsides under the trees where verdure had pushed up through the brown covering of last year's leaves. By last evening the grass had turned green in village lawns, and the cherry tree below my window across the track bore swollen buds. Nature's green had lain dormant long enough. It was pushing up to take over the earth.

Yesterday was Good Friday. When I hurried up to the Squire's to dress and brush out my new permanent before supper, Mrs. Woodward had the communion bread cut in a plate and the wine set out beside it. An evening candlelight communion service was held in the Methodist Church, which many of the folks from the country attended. Some of them we hadn't seen all winter. As we bowed reverently in the dim candlelight, I thought that this communion was in one way like spring housecleaning. We brought all the wrongs of the winter to leave at the altar and started out again with a clean life.

April 7, 1947

Easter was warm and sunny and gave us the longed-for opportunity to wear spring clothes. Only the merchants' wives had entirely new outfits, which we enjoyed seeing as much as they enjoyed wearing them. The rest of us bought one or two new pieces to go with last spring's costume, satisfied if we were presentable. The important thing was that we could at last shed the soiled, dark, heavy clothes of winter for thinner, cleaner, prettier ones.

Rev. Kooser was busy all day christening babies and holding Easter services at his three charges. At the evening one in our town, McFarland and his English bride were taken into the church and the babies of two young men just out of the navy were christened. The babies were dressed in the latest of pink and white baby clothes, bobbing in surprise when the pastor took each into his arms and placed a wet hand on their downy heads. Later, while he preached his sermon, they grew restless, and their mothers tiptoed out with them. I, too, in mind, slipped away from his earnestness, thinking of those even in our own little town who had forgotten or to whom Easter had no significance. How was the Church's influence in this world ever to be more than a drop in the bucket when there were so many even here that it did not reach?

April 14, 1947
    I broke my routine yesterday by taking a trip to Pittsburgh with my family. I saw the steel mills and the coal barges being paddled down the river through the eyes of my small nephew. I enjoyed the bustle and the hum of the city, and the beauty of the flower show, with my niece. Each was seeing it for the first time. We lingered in glass-domed rooms of pink and blue hyacinths, yellow tulips combined with purple potted plants. There was even a New England room at the flower show with blooming dogwood and white birch and a cabin glimpsed through the trees.

I wished I could bring to them a Pennsylvania room filled with the wild flowers I can find in a mile's walk here as each week brings a different group into bloom. There would be the tiny pink blossoms of trailing arbutus, evergreen ferns and the waxy white petals of the bloodroot first of all. Then violets, yellow, purple, white, under a tall beech and a white dogwood. There would be white trillium, fragile white Dutchman's britches, yellow dagger's tongue, pink wild geranium. And they would be followed by wild pink phlox, yellow and rose lady slippers and fragrant pink honeysuckle. Each one of them has or will be in bloom this spring, but I have had little time to get out to find them.

April 16, 1947

I did not get out to see the trillium. All week I have been looking out my office windows at the pink magnolia tree blooming across the river in Billy Rafferty's yard. I knew by it that it was time for the trillium in my favorite ravine, and when I locked the station yesterday there was time to visit them.

I followed the route Annie Williams used to travel across the two railroad bridges and up the steep path at the end of the high bridge across the river. Then there is a mossy path branching off of Annie's to a deep ravine where a brook murmurs softly over the stones at the bottom. On both sides of the ravine the steep banks are covered with white trillium growing out of the brown leaf mold, small white lilies reaching their heads up in the dim woods toward the light. It is a spot I love. Sitting there under the straight, high trees, listening to the brook and feasting my eyes on the white flowers, all the little exasperations of life melt away and are forgotten. There is more peace there than in any other sanctuary I know.

April 23, 1947   The cherry tree across the track below my office window burst into bloom in the night and is bedecked with white blossoms this morning. The cherry trees across the river are in bloom, and two red-bud trees are holding up pink branches against the white ones.

April 30, 1947

I have been housecleaning my station. I have brushed the dust off the walls and stovepipe, washed the windows, cleaned the window shades and polished the desks. The California poppies that re-seed themselves are up in the small bed beside the station, and the Shirley poppy seedlings that lived through the zero cold by the walk are now sturdy plants. Poppies are always a good choice for spring, because they scorn spring frosts and go right on growing. We are hoping there will be no more frosts this spring, for even the apple trees are coming in blossom.

May 10, 1947

When May Day arrived, the apple trees were loaded with bloom. I saw a bluebird and a butterfly with yellow wings edged in black. But before the week was over, there came a wind from the northwest with a beating rain, and we built fires again to keep warm. Then the clouds disappeared from the sky one night and left it icily clear. The next morning the frost was thick and white. It is thought about half the fruit crop is killed. We know, however, that at least a part of it was saved by the small, green cherries and apples we see – we hope enough to cover extreme needs.

I am putting my office in order in preparation to turning it over to Richard Martin for two weeks while I go down to the Railroad Center and help my mother clean house.

May 26, 1947

For two weeks I forgot my little town. For two weeks I scraped dirty paper off walls and pasted clean paper on in place of it, cut grass, scrubbed porches, painted floors. I climbed up and down stepladders until every muscle in my body was sore. I'd drop in an easy chair when the supper dishes were done, exhausted, and more aware then ever why a woman never gets as much done in a house in one day as people think she should.

For two weeks my ears were assailed with the steady roar of traffic as soon as I opened my front door. The warning screech of an ambulance siren, the blast of a fire whistle, the hum of an airplane motor were common noises no one bothered about. For two weeks people passed by my door I didn't know and who didn't know me. The two weeks is over. Yesterday afternoon my brother-in-law drove me back here to my little town, and I began to relax as soon as the car climbed up in the mountains.

The woods were heavy with foliage. The grass had grown so high, our little town looked shaggy, and my first mental note as I passed my station was that I would have to ask Jud to cut the railroad bank. The Squire and Mrs. Woodward roused from a Sunday nap to greet me, and I sat with them a while catching up on the news of a fortnight. David was married to a girl from South Carolina and was bringing her home for Memorial Day. A couple of our neighbors were lawing over the ownership of a house. An old bachelor who lived with his brother and sister on a place out of town had killed himself so he wouldn't have to go to the hospital. And, most important at the moment, the Baccalaureate sermon for the high school graduates was to be preached this Sunday at the Methodist Church. We had better eat our supper and be there early, or we wouldn't get a seat.

I sat in a whispering congregation, facing a flower-bedecked altar, watching and recognizing each proud pair of parents as they came in and found seats. Many of them had come in from the country. A lady looked back at me and smiled. Another nodded from across the aisle. The principle and his wife were sitting near the front. The Methodist minister had gone up to the pulpit and the Baptist one was on hand for the invocation. The pianist sat down at the piano, and the church orchestra began to play. The folding doors of this Sunday School room were pushed aside. Ten boys and girls, clad in caps and gowns, marched slowly down the aisles to their seats in the front row.

The May twilight fell as we listened to the preacher's solemn words to the graduates. I don't remember what he said; perhaps I wasn't always listening. I was thinking that it was good to be here, and I would liked to have graduated from a place like this myself.

May 31, 1947

The most important business news Richard left me was that a man named Kingsley, a coal stripper, had leased coal up on Kentuck and was proposing to bulldoze a road down the mountain and load it on Torrence. This far Torrence had been to me what a red flag is supposed to be to a bull. Just a taunt. There it lays, 20 car-lengths of good siding track used for nothing whatsoever, beyond the high railroad bridge where there is no road and no possible way for a truck to get to it. Once upon a time an old mine track bridged gorges and tunneled a mountain to get to it, but all that wooden construction work is now rotten and fallen in. If I had had that nice piece of track where trucks could have reach it, I would have had all the coal business in town. A road to Torrence was the kind of news that made me really pick up my ears. I have been getting information and getting in touch with railroad officials all week, securing permission for Kingsley to load there.

On Wednesday evening, I attended the commencement exercises of the high school graduates. They had Mr. Weaver from Meadow Run, who once was a Pittsburgh florist, decorate the school auditorium in dogwood, snowballs, and rhododendron. The valedictorian was Frank Dull, the oldest of those three bright boys Gene Simpson's wife had left when she died last fall. He spoke on the subject of Broader Vision. The clergyman following him, who had come from the Railroad Center to make the principal address, said he was much impressed by the young man's words. The next day Frank was back on his paper route.

I watched Frank that evening depositing my Pittsburgh Press in the bill box and wondered how broad his vision really was and how far it would take him. A broader vision was what this town needed. A third of its citizens were on direct relief rolls with a million dollars worth of beauty outside their windows. Frank had no training to enable him to see that vision, had no money with which to make it materialize and no one to help him. He would have to follow the standardized routes to earn a living, and I feared high purpose would fade as the road grew long and tiresome.

I could have told him that even if he hung on to his vision it was only one-third of what it takes to succeed. The other two-thirds are work and the guts to go on in the face of defeat. Many of us have come to the place where we know with absolute finality that we cannot win, that not one tiny bit of our dream can ever come true, but we still go on. Because if you stop, you go backwards. Graduation speakers don't like to touch on such unpleasant subjects; they seem afraid to bring our young folks down to earth. However, the U.S. Army had no such qualms, and their cynical G.I.'s won their part of a world war. Some of them didn't return, but they won. Now their comrades are trying to find an easier road to success and to win the peace, but the Lord warned us 2,000 years ago that it is on the easier roads that you lose your soul. We who are older have no inspiring message for the young. We can only tell them that you just have to keep on trying, and praying. You even have to try when you know it is utterly useless. If you stop, you'll be down with the hobos.

Yesterday was Memorial Day. None of the railroad gangs were working, and I was alone at my station with only an occasional train passing. The day was chilly, and I kept a fire alive for warmth. City folks who came our way with plans to spend the day outdoors left their bathing suits in their cars, put on sweaters, and walked in the sun. Townsfolk had cut the grass on their lots in the cemetery and planted potted flowers on the graves earlier in the week. Yesterday they rested and entertained whatever visitors came to call. David brought the expected bride home, and Mrs. Woodward reported that her granddaughter is a quiet girl with a southern accent who had been raised on a farm.

June 10, 1947

It is summer. There were some cool days at first, till June finally got the best of that northwest wind; there were some heavy rains to ensure ample water supply during the heat, and then the sun came out. The sun, which had been shut away from us for so long! The sun, scorching down into the skin. I worked a half hour in it after closing hour, digging a ditch to lead surface water away from a flower bed, and my face was livid, my clothes soggy. People wiped the sweat off their brows and wondered ruefully why they couldn't stand a little heat. The answer is obvious. We have not known the real summer sun for nine months.

We love it. It has brought our town back to the way we like it most. There is heavy foliage wherever we look, hemming us in with a wall of green. Velvety roses bloom on the lawns, and the large, bending heads of peonies. An orange and black oriole sits in the big oak by the Methodist Church and calls three monotonous notes all day long. Blue-gray swallows with rose breasts and forked tails stunt in front of the station, building nests and raising families on any protected ledge. Children run half-naked under the sun, free at last of school. My poppies are blooming profusely, red, white and pink ones, and Labor stops, a little pale but sober, to admire them. There has to be something nice about a man who likes flowers.

When I dress for supper my room is so hot I have to leave the door ajar to coax a breath of air between it and the open windows. The sun is slipping down toward the horizon by then, and I can hear the birds all about twittering in glad relief. On my way to Ray's I see soft, bluish shadows come on the thick, green wall of trees at the end of the street where the river drops over the falls. Men who have eaten early are gathered on the corners, talking. Some sit on Bob Locke's store porch, or on the bench by the barbershop where they can watch the youngsters in the river and get the benefit of any stray breeze from the water.

After the evening meal, I walk beside the falls while bats dart above me in the twilight. Soon the June dark is gleaming with hundreds of fireflies, and I sit with Della and Edith Stewart on their wide porch, looking up at the millions of stars and talking at random above the undertone of the falls till long after the hoarse voice of the daisies on the B&O tell us the Capitol Limited and the New York to Chicago Pullman train have sped by, and the time is close midnight.

There will be other winds from the northwest. There will be rains and cool evenings that will make me snuggle deep in my rose-colored topper when I go to Ray's. But it will still be summer. For a few precious months we will live close in the outdoors, and even work will be a vacation in contrast to our life in winter. We will wake in the mornings with the sun in our eyes and a song on our lips, because we are as glad we're alive as the birds outside, singing over the dew-sprinkled landscape. We will scorch under the midday sun. We will rest on our porches while a pale pink sunset turns to blue dusk, and we'll linger a while to map the star-studded sky in quiet and sweet peace before we go up to rooms that quickly cool as we drop into dreamless slumber.

We will get so much fun out of living close to the outdoors that we will forget about the radio and the cold wars of the atom bomb. We will be aware in the back of our mind that nefarious schemes are afoot wherever there are men. We will be close enough to God's earth these next months to realize that He is greater than any group of men. There is protection and a way to live in peace if enough men in enough lands would desire peace and pray for it sincerely.

If they would. Should Christians do something about that? Some warm Sunday morning when the little girls in their best dresses are wriggling in their seats while their Sunday School teacher talks and they absently watch a vagrant breeze through the open church door stirring the leaves of the oak and bending the heads of the wheat on the hilltop field, I look for a member of the Men's Bible Class to ask that question. Or maybe it will be asked as the stained glass windows strain the twilight on a half-dozen gathered for mid-week prayer meeting. Should there not be a movement started, a sort of a chain of prayers, for peace upon this earth? How would you go about beginning such an effort? Would the big churches help us as well as the little ones? Really pray, that is, not just a nicey-nice cooperation. How could we go about starting a prayer for peace that would reach around the world?

Not even Squire Woodward has lost his zest for life this spring. He grows thinner and has trouble keeping the upper plate of his false teeth in place, but he keeps busy. He has sold two tracts of his farming land to young farmers so that he won't have to keep the buildings and fences in repair, but he has kept one for his livestock. When he was in my office this week getting a deed typed, he said that one track was giving him trouble enough, that a dog had attacked his sheep, killed one and injured several, including his best ewe – the one who had surprised him this spring with triplet lambs. He had made two round trips to River Junction the previous day, one to buy nine head of cattle for $500. They returned later to weigh them. He said Flora was sure he was going to lose his money, but you got to risk a little to gain anything.

Mrs. Woodward's fearfulness comes from ill health. There have been numerous minor ills added to the rheumatism in her crippled knees. Lee's death, too, will be a scar on both hearts as long as they live. The Squire has learned to accept the grievances that life has laid upon him, but Flora's heartbreak will not always let her rest. Sometimes these quiet nights I hear her walking about. The next morning she will tell me she was nervous and went downstairs to eat some crackers and milk.

June 21, 1947

The WM helped the unemployment situation a great deal in our little town this spring. The rock gang has hired two men from Sugar Loaf. That gang has been blasting the rock bank east of town back farther from the track for several months. A grouting gang working west of town has been running cement into the fills along the river bank to hold them. Judd has hired three new men, two of them discharged soldiers, for his regular track maintenance gang. Neil has hired three former soldiers and one high school graduate for summer work in the signal department. Unfortunately, all of it is summer work of a temporary nature. Good, permanent jobs are not to be had. That is what is hurting our town the most. Each year the best of the younger generation leaves to find work offering the hope of advancement. Therefore, we do not have the young blood we need in our political offices and other organizations.

We had a motion picture at the Methodist Church this week. A mission worker from one of the mining towns brought DeMille's silent version of the story of Jesus, "The King of Kings." The church was filled with people from town and the country who seemed to enjoy it, their silver offering to cover the cost amounting to $30. To me, the old picture seemed overdone, the sets too elaborate. All the players seemed to be over-acting except Christ who, on the contrary, lacked the fire and passion of Jesus. Since then the ladies have been wondering of it would be possible to bring motion pictures and other good shows to town, but the difficulties seem insurmountable in such a small community.

A man brings a portable motion picture projector on Saturday evenings and puts on a show in the school auditorium, but he must show pictures in 16mm film. Only small companies with poor stories and unknown actors make this small size, and, consequently, a really good picture is never shown. The cost of a motion picture theater is too great for anyone to attempt to bring good pictures to town. A hillbilly radio show comes to the school auditorium sometimes, but their music and patter is of such poor grade very few folks from town will attend them. One wonders at the intelligence of a radio station that will book such poorly educated groups, usually young folks who have not finished high school and who have had very little training in music. Their radio programs cater to the uneducated in remote places, and our complaint is that they lower the taste of these folks. Young mothers and their children, with such drivel constantly in their ears, never learn to appreciate good music or intelligent entertainment.

June 30, 1947   The hottest part of the summer is here. The days are sultry, the evenings beautiful. A big, round June moon this week has turned our town into a fairyland of beauty each night. When you cross the bridge, the glassy river reflects the yellow ball. The shaggy pine that hangs over Commercial Street is silhouetted black against the moonlight. And the road by the falls and out to Castle Rock is a silver highway with a misty hill at the bend of the river.

On Sundays, Western Pennsylvanians pour into our town bumper to bumper. The river is filled with them all the way through town and down past Long Rocks. The park teams with picnickers, and Long Rocks is covered with them. Young folks sun on the flat rocks down there and dive in smooth, deep green water. Old folks sit under umbrellas or the shade of trees, while children run about merrily, the falls breaking in white in the distance above them. When dark settles thick along the river, they go back to their towns. On Monday afternoon after work, I have Long Rocks to myself while Western Pennsylvania does its laundry and talks about the strike.

Of course there are many strikers. My embargo file is filling up again with minor altercations in plants in various sections of the country. They strike, and I put in an embargo. In a couple of weeks or a couple of months the workers come to terms with the management, and I take it out. It causes no ripple here. When Western Pennsylvania talks about "the strike," they mean the one the coal miners are threatening to come out on.

The miners are taking a two-week vacation. During that period, their contract with the government will have expired, and they will have to make a new one with the mine owners. We wait for contrary men on both sides of the issue, arguing over the money in coal, to reach an agreement that will give us prosperity for another year.

Meantime, the church people trained their Sunday School students for Children's Day. The Baptists put on their exercises the evening of last Sunday a week, and the Methodists celebrated Children's Day last night. All the parents and grandparents and many of the rest of us were there. There's something about a small child, freshly washed and prettily dressed, standing up there in front of the congregation fidgeting nervously, reciting and sometimes forgetting a few simple verses, that makes us laugh with a lump in our throat. It's not just that they are children with cute ways, but because they thrill over such simple pleasures, are so full of expectancy and have known no disillusionment.

The pianist and the primary teacher outdid themselves on the program last evening. They had the church decorated in white hydrangeas and pink rambler roses, and the children on tiptoe with excitement. The tiny tots came first. There was Walker's grandchildren and Lohr's granddaughter – with Lohr in church for the first time this year. There was an illegitimate little blonde who had her mommie and her mommie's new boyfriend there to hear her sing. The English bride's small daughter always barges in like Churchill, but last night she looked at the room of faces and was quelled to a murmur. So was the teacher's young Patrick, with his pompadour of tow hair standing straight up.

There were individual recitations, and a slender girl played a piano solo. The intermediate girls in colorful paper dresses were in a play. The tall girls, clothed in white, were in a pantomime with the pianist's daughter singing softly in the background. There was even an exercise called "dropping pennies," which the children sang while the collection was being taken – and which Rev. Kooser said he hoped we wouldn't take too literally these days of inflation.

Then he pronounced the benediction, and we shook hands happily and walked through the dusk to our homes. I accompanied Mrs. Martin to her high porch in the dark, where we sat and looked down on the lights of the town and the streamlined passenger trains winding below us on the B&O tracks.

July 10, 1947

The Fourth of July was a perfect day with a hot sun and a clear, green river, the cars of swimmers and picnickers coming to us in a steady stream. For a day or a weekend of nature's blessed healing, they could relax in the outdoors. Then they have to return to their hot towns and their problems. We watched them absently piling out of their cars and making their way to the river in every imaginable type of bathing suit. We sat in the cool of the Stewart girls' porch with her brother, a New York attorney, and his gracious wife, who had just arrived for a visit.

Now the skies are clearing from a half week of pouring rain, and the river is full of mud. No one cares. no one wants to swim anyway. John Lewis has signed a contract, too. He got $1.20 more a day for an hour's less work for his miners, increased the welfare fund to 10 cents a ton, got them a vacation with pay, the federal safety code adopted and permission to organize the mine foreman. For a year everyone can make plans. They can begin building that new home, or get a new roof or a bathroom for the old one, a refrigerator or an electric stove, and arrange to pay for them with monthly payments. They will have steady work for a year. The track-man who maintains the railroad's roadbed and the woodsman who cuts the mine props will earn a much smaller salary than the miner, but he can look forward to regular employment, because there will be a steady flow of business.

July 24, 1947   A wind came down from the northwest this week. I have been burning old tariffs in the stove to take off the chill. The wind isn't as cold, though, as the hotel. They really have it in for me over there. A petition was filed last Friday at the County Commissioner's office that will enable the town to vote in the September primary on the question of whether or not the citizens want beer and liquor sold is this borough. The hotel crowd says it is my fault the question has come up.

It was the fault of a number of us. John Snyder first openly voiced the complaints about the leniency of the hotel management that had caused me to leave in the winter. He voiced them to Democrat friends and said the "Church people ought to do something about it," pointing out that they could vote on local option this year if they wanted. The church people had been criticized once before for not making the issue a political one. This time they decided they would give the citizens the opportunity to decide at the polls, and they asked me to help gather the signatures on a petition so that the question could be put up to vote. I agreed. Mrs. Alice Locke's daughter, Gwen Waters, said she would gather signatures if I would help her, and she also asked Edith Stewart. We had to have 25 percent of the voters at the last election. That was 33. We had 47 names on our petition when the Squire left it in Uniontown to be filed.

Privately, I was not keen about my job, although I didn't let that be known. A few years previous I had refused to collect signatures despite being both a Methodist and the treasurer of the WCTU. I was also the agent for the WM, eating the only good meal I got then at the hotel, and I didn't want to be drawn into the bitterness of such a controversy. Furthermore, I didn't want to ruin a man's business, and I feared the hotel would have a hard time existing without its barroom. I knew it could be done, but it would take some of that broad vision Frank talked about and that our saloon-keepers didn't have. And I didn't like the idea of punishing the one man in the borough who was making an honest attempt to fill the public's demand for rooms and meals when roadside stand in the township could serve liquor without any pretense of being a hotel. I felt, whatever regulations were made, should be statewide and make every man observe the same law.

This time, however, the demand for a cleanup was statewide.   The liquor interests have gone too far in their campaign to make this a nation of drunkards. They have tried to put bills through the legislature to sell beer in food stores and in clubs without any regulation whatsoever. The bills failed by too narrow a margin. It is time we woke up our legislature. Every restaurant in our big towns is given over to the selling of liquor with only a little food served in the back, and as a result, the newspaper headlines are filled with violence. The drys suddenly moved in a body, and local option elections are being held all over the state. I could not turn down a challenge like that. I could not forget the useless days last winter our returned soldiers spent around the oilcloth-covered tables drinking. I could not forget that I had been contributing editor of The Messenger and would be expected to have enough guts to take my stand with the drys.

But privately I think the campaign is too radical and quite likely to lose. The Anti-Saloon League is heading it, sending out the petition blanks and literature asking that the sale of both liquor and beer be banned and that, if the communities will do that, the State will respect their wishes and also take out the state liquor stores located in the large towns. The wets have come back quite regularly with the argument that that would bring back moon shining and bootlegging. It would seem a better idea to me to ban the sale of liquor except at state stores and sell only beer at hotels, stands, and restaurants. If that could be accomplished and still stricter laws of handling alcohol were wanted, they could be worked out gradually as we gradually weaned our people away from alcoholic beverages. It seems to me more progress could be made gradually than to attempt to jump from a sopping wet state to a bone-dry one.

But I am lined up with the drys, and there I will stay in the minds of the townsfolk. A list of us who signed the petition was tacked profanely to the barroom wall, and all sorts of threats have been made against us. The women who frequent the barroom began running in my station shouting hysterical imprecations. One of them told me she was just as good as I was. I told her I hope that was true and shut the door with a crooked smile. I was thinking that she probably was, in the beginning, and that it is not impossible for me, also, to make mistakes and misjudge situations, which was what caused her downfall. I have no fondness for the place I have achieved as the leader of this campaign, set up for the opposition to try to pull down.

July 28, 1947   July heat came back over the weekend, and the river was glassy green again Sunday afternoon when I brought my lame sister up on the local passenger train for an hour in the cool water and a picnic lunch on the rocks. She returned home with the Rev. and Mrs. Kooser after the evening church service. But even in that brief period I could not get away from the coal business. An attorney who had brought his family swimming had stopped in to see the Squire about a certain Pittsburgh promoter, who wanted right of way across the attorney's and to a siding he proposed to build on the site east of the station. The Squire knew nothing about him, and I only knew that he talked a little too fast to be dependable and that my land-poor friends in town were hoping against hope the business would materialize. They wanted to exchange their coal land for the old-age security royalty payments would bring them.

I have more calls for sidings than I have land to put them on. Another man also wants the site east of the station. As for Kingsley, who is planning to load on Torrance, he has decided to build his road to the 20-car length siding, not down the mountain, but upon the old mine track that originally led to that siding. That means he must resurface the track, fill in the gorges, and bulldoze a road around the mountain the mine track tunneled under. So far he just has the brush cut. In the back of my mind, I am wondering the advisability of all this.

In the back of our mind all of us are wondering. What is the future of coal? Throughout the war it was black diamonds, indeed. Diamond dust to the stripper who shoveled off his almost unusable top layer and shipped it to Italy where it had to be mixed with something to burn it. "Bug dust" to the sarcastic men who dumped it into the coal hoppers. But the railroad officials say the stripper's day is over when Europe begins mining her own coal. That is why they are not interested in building track. Only the strippers with very good coal and the small deep mine with good coal extremely efficient operations will be able to survive. There is more coal being mined in America, they say, than America needs, and the big mines will fill America's coal order.

It is feared even the big mines will not have enough coal orders to keep them working full time. It is feared that America is overproduced. There will be more refrigerators and stoves and breakfast sets and automobiles than will be needed; that will mean less steel; that will mean less coal; that will mean less steel orders from the railroads; and the combination will mean less prosperity for the East. The beautiful lady buying an expensive jewel, the young dude buying a swanky auto, may be so far removed from the coal business they don't know where their money is coming from. But we know. We're watching and wondering. Officials told me in the winter of '46 that my shippers wouldn't be able to sell coal by June. A year later there is more coal activity than ever. Europe can't seem to get going. But it will mine coal again. When? What will happen when it does?

I am still hopeful. I am hopeful that civilization will expand and that America will sell to it. I am even hopeful that, along about the time we sell modern plumbing to Tibet, our town council will find a way of putting a city water and sewer system in our little town.

July 30, 1947   The Squire was 84 years old yesterday. Heretofore, his birthday was always celebrated with a chicken supper at Lee's, but this year was very different. Hearts that are healed only on the outside cannot stand a celebration. I slipped a handkerchief into a birthday card and left it on the kitchen table the night before so he would get it when he got up the morning of his birthday to put the tea kettle on. He thanked me when I came down for breakfast and went off to the barn and then to Sugar Loaf to see about his livestock. In the late afternoon, Ella brought over a plate of his favorite fudge and left it for him to find when he returned.

This is the month the rhododendron blooms. Rambler roses were masses of red, pink, and white on fences and trellises the first two weeks of July. I had a double row of hollyhocks at the foot of the railroad bank most of the month, but in the woods the rhododendron grows in every shady spot and spills over the cliffs and the rocks by the river. It is covered now with big clusters of pinkish white blossoms.

This last week of the month has been very warm, and there has been a great round moon at night. I spent last evening talking to Della and Edith Stewart on their cool porch above the falls, little dreaming the barroom crowd was taking the opportunity to vent their spits on me. But when I came to work this morning I found all the blooming flowers in my bed beside the track – phlox, petunia, balsam – had been pulled up, and two empty beer cans were left in their place.

August 5, 1947   The sky was such a deep blue today.
The sun burned bright hot against the skin, and the river was a
cool green down below the falls where I went after work to
bathe. When I would crawl out of the water and lie against a
slanting rock, I was facing the tallest of all the pines, the one
growing out of the river rock with only a topmost crest of
branches, silhouetted like a mast against the green of the hill
and the blue of the sky. The goldenrod is coming in bloom by
the river and waist-high yellow daisies. The pink heads of the
Joe-pie weed can be seen along the road and the purple ones of
ironweed.

          Along the railroad track there are a couple varieties of
orchid-colored thistles in bloom and farther down the
blackberries and elderberries are getting ripe. Beyond them the
woods are very dense. In all our flowerbeds the zinnias,
cosmos, and other annuals are blooming in profusion.

Tuesday, Aug. 12, 1947
          This month thus far has been filled with wrangling, all
of it brewing for a long time but coming to a head in the last
two weeks. There was the argument about the high school
teachers. The citizens declared the two young ladies who had
helped teach the high school could not come back. They were
too giddy. They dated their boy students. They did not enforce
discipline, and they wasted the taxpayer's money and the
serious student's time. The county school officials said the girls
had good diplomas, that teachers were hard to get, and that the
citizens were a bunch of fussy old women. The citizens
reminded them that an illegitimate child had been born to one
of the schoolgirls last year, and the same thing happened the
year before. They said the school needed the influence of more
sober leadership.

Squire Woodward is president of the school board, and while he was trying to find a middle-of-the-road decision in that argument he found himself embroiled in another. As trustee of the Methodist Church, he was in the middle of an altercation about repairs to the church. Money had been raised to roof and paint the building, but one faction said the roofing material was of poor quality and refused to allow it to be put on. The other faction ignored them and contracted to have the building roofed with it. Worse still, they contracted to have the church sprayed instead of hand painted, and one of the opposing factions was a painter who needed work. The contracting faction was obdurate. They said the building was badly weather beaten, and they wanted to force the paint into all the cracks with a power-spraying machine. The opposition, which included all the Lockes except Charlie's family, washed their hands of the whole thing and refused to attend any type of church service held by the Methodists. They were even down on the preacher because he sided and aided the faction doing the construction.

The Methodists, the contracting faction, and the rest of us tried to go on having church as usual, but the Lockes are a big group, and everyone was uncomfortably aware of the empty seats. The Squire made mild attempts to remind both groups that they were Christians and should be willing to meet and pray together, but his suggestions fell on deaf ears. The contractor, however, had his contract, and the church now has a new blue roof, a copper peak on its spire, and two coats of gleaming white paint. The contractor also has his money. When we will have all our congregation back together again is uncertain, but they have grudgingly admitted that the church looks nice. They say it's not going to last and darkly predict that we have thrown our money away.

And since that isn't enough arguing, the Civic Club, of whom I am the home improvement committee, has found itself the brunt of a lot of criticism through no fault of its own. We just asked the power company who owns the plot by the falls to beautify it to the extent of sowing some grass on it and building some barriers to keep automobiles from driving on it. They replied that they would kill the border of poison ivy around the edge and cut some brush that was blocking the view of the falls and were willing to allow the public on their land to enjoy the scenery, but if we wanted any grass planted, we would have to plant it ourselves. As for barriers, they said we would have to dig in stones. Someone might fall off a fence, and they would be sued.

Old Mr. Bremner, who owns the lodge at the entrance of town, was enthusiastic. Being a member of Council, he had the rocks brought at once, at Council's expense. The trouble was the idea got bawled up by someone, and too many rocks were brought at too great an expense. Jim Robinson hollered that the taxpayers' money was being wasted. Along about that time, the various folks who had been trying to manage the affair bowed out of the picture and bowed me into it.

I have been looking over the situation with a rueful eye. Obviously, I am going to have to accomplish something if I am to placate the citizens, and it looks like that something is going to take all my spare time for the rest of the fall. I will have to beg a truck and pay men out of our $60 of civic club funds for a half -dozen truckloads of earth that grass will grow on. It will have to be raked, rolled, and sowed. Ungainly boulders will have to be arranged and dug into a neat barrier, and the irritating ones up in front of Jim's rolled back along the riverbank and painted to mark the parking space. A ditch will have to be dug to lead the water from the steep Sugar Loaf road off the plot we want to grass, and a flowerbed should be made behind the wall. That $60 can be stretched over all that only if I do the light work myself as well as supervising the job. As I filed all that in my mind, it occurred to me that it was I, in the first place, who had carried to the club Della Stewart's suggestion that the plot be beautiful. I who had planned to spend my spare time in the river and the woods till winter closed in again. I am always playing such kinds of tricks on myself.

August 19, 1947

This has been the rainiest August we have ever known. Perhaps I notice it more because Kingsley is trying to build a road to Torrence, and the rains are making it exasperatingly difficult. His road is deep in mud even where it is being built on the slate bed of the old mine track, and you sink to your ankles where he is filling in the gorges. He has felled trees and made them into culverts over the streams then filled in with earth banked high and wide for a truck to traverse. It has been no small job. It is a lot worse job with wet, soggy clay that doesn't dry from one rain till another. Even so, Kingsley's men have made a fine road that isn't at too steep a grade where it crosses the mountain and comes down into the last long ravine and onto his loading dock at Torrance.

While Kingsley's men build road, a country schoolteacher by the name of Ida Bailey and I have been penetrating Greenbrier mountain beyond its coal strip. We have had to leave the paved road and follow lanes to remote houses where only a country schoolteacher would agree to take an automobile. Our errand has been to complete the job of collecting the data for the service record we are publishing of our soldiers. We didn't want to overlook the ones in this township who came from these mountain farms, so Ida has been heading her car into the hills with me beside her on free August evenings.

We found mud lanes sloshing in stagnant water with a green screen of trees and bushes bent down to hide what lay ahead as the car scraped against their wet leaves and felt its way forward. Usually Ida knew where she was going. To my surprise, she told me she not only had taught these one-room schools but had boarded through bitterly cold winters in these uncomfortable homes, firing the blizzards back from her schoolroom, wading knee-deep snow in the lanes.

"I didn't have much of a bed, but I got enough to eat, such as it was," she laughed.

I told her she not only deserved a raise, she deserved a medal.

She stopped to see the mother of a girl she had once taught who had been burned to death after she had gone to town to work and attend high school. The mother, her husband and sons had just come in from the small fields behind the old house. The mother said they had planned to go to prayer meeting, but they were too tired. She still choked up when she spoke of her daughter.

We landed at the prayer meeting instead. It was in a pleasanter farm home that had once had paint on it. There was a grass yard with a lilac and some rose bushes, too. We didn't find the boy we were looking for but all the women in the mountain, from children to an aged lady, and a sprinkling of men, also, had gathered in the living room to sing hymns by the light of an oil lamp and listen to the reading of the scriptures. Their leader was an able gentleman doing home mission work for a Sunday school union. He said he confined his work to those off the paved highways.

Another evening we drove up to a large, weather-beaten house sitting in the middle of its fields on the top of the mountain. To me it was less lonely and impoverished because of the view it commanded. But it was growing dusk, and the house had that kind of silence that made you feel its inmates were sizing you up. We went in hesitatingly. The yellow light of an oil lamp in the big, dark kitchen cast only a feeble gleam on what seemed to be a room of overalled, unshaven men. Then we saw there were women, too, a stout smiling, gray-haired lady, her daughter, a still younger girl and a baby.

As Ida explained our errand with the usual composure of a teacher, the men relented from their first stiff suspicion and began to laugh and talk. They lit the oil lamp in the cluttered living room and showed us snapshots of all of Europe, especially the tourist spots the GI of the family had been able to visit while overseas. He was in his thirties. All of the men were keen and witty, if bearded, the women friendly. There was no trouble there about getting the photos and records we needed.

Nor was there any trouble at the three-room shack we reached one evening by following a steep trail through the dark to their oil light. There were two sons there. One was a Marine from the Pacific Theater with four battle stars and a Purple Heart. The other had viewed the same hell from a battleship. They were now working with their father at a small sawmill. These men were bearded, too, but they were handsome fellows whose heads almost touched the low, dark ceiling. Showing me his discharge papers seemed to get under the Marine's skin. As I strained my eyes beside the feeble light and wrote at the kitchen table he walked outdoors restlessly. His mother whispered he was still pretty nervous. He had wanted to re-enlist, but he had been turned down because of his wounds.

Being a woman, the outstanding place in my memory was the mountain shanty we met the French bride. It was set up on stilts on the hillside. There was neither yard nor garden, just three rooms of rough boards blackened by age. Stains on the porch floor indicated someone in the household chewed snuff and wasn't careful where they spat. The glimpse of the kitchen linoleum I caught from the porch showed it was worn brown and none too clean. The soldier, his bride, and their toddling daughter lived with his parents and some brothers and sisters. I couldn't imagine where they all slept or what sort of an existence it would be in winter.

The soldier had been Ida's student, and his mother welcomed her warmly. She told Ida that the French girl had been an only child who lived in a comfortable home near Rheims, and Jim had met her while he was working at a PX there. She said the girl had had to work for the Germans during the occupation and had learned to speak German. Then, since Jim couldn't learn French, the girl had learned English. She said her daughter-in-law got lots of letters from her mother in France.

The girl stood silent. She had a pretty face and long red curls, but her silk print dress was soiled, and her figure growing heavy from starchy food. Jim's mother asked her, for our benefit, which she liked best, Germany, France, or America.

The French girl looked at us, embarrassed. "France," she answered with an apologetic laugh.

I looked up and smiled. "You'll like America better when you get a home of your own."

Her husband explained to me that that might be a long time yet. He said he and his father were working in a mine near the County Seat, driving a 60-mile round-trip in the only modern thing they owned, their automobile. I knew that meant he was spending a lot of money traveling to and from his work. He said he didn't know where he could find a house for a separate home.

This week I was told Jim did find a house, after all, near the mines. I keep wondering what his wife's surroundings are now, and if she will learn to like America.

The last trip we made was to decaying Stonersville, where Don and his wife and baby son, and Paul and his wife and little girl, were living in two of the better houses. Wife and house were as clean as the surroundings made it possible. Both men had a week's stubble on their face. Daily shaves are for men with plumbing. Don had a patch over his eye, which, I learned later, he received at River Junction after a few drinks. He had boasted he'd whip any man in the crowd, then any two men. And he did.

Don showed us where he had crossed the Rhine at Remagen. Paul's leg was scarred from a wound received as he advanced through Germany.

August 30, 1947   August has continued rainy to the very end. Kingsley is discouraged and wondering if the rain will ever quit. He loaded his first car of coal yesterday, but his road is still a lob lolly of mud. His stripper says every time they pick up a stone they find a spring of water. The local men working on the project claim Kingsley does everything wrong, not enough drains, not enough stone, that he tries to put a top on the road when the road is wet and the top sinks in the mud, that when the road is dry enough for a top he tries to get trucks over it to load coal instead.

One thing is certain and that is that that road cost him a lot of money, and he is going to have to load a lot of coal to justify it. I am wondering if he will be able to do that. He thinks winter is going to be the ideal time for coal stripping, that the ground will freeze and he won't be bothered with water. I think he will have snow and ice on that steep mountain to combat before he gets to his own road, plus all the ills zero brings, from frozen ports to broken machinery. Also that he spends too much time being optimistic over the hotel bar. When the ground freezes as hard as these strippers want it, the weather will be extremely cold, and they will have other troubles to worry about. Furthermore, we have no more extreme cold than we have extreme heat, six weeks at most. And when the ground thaws, Kingsley's trucks will sink to their hubs.

However, everyone associated with the project thinks he is going to get rich quick. The old mine company wants four dollars a car for the privilege of allowing Kingsley to use the road he built over their marshy slate fills, rotted trestles, and fallen-in tunnel. The men who own the coal he is to strip are charging him a monthly rental without any allowance for the bad weather we always get, and the car shortage the newspapers tell us is to go with it. Everyone wants to be sure of his cut whether Kingsley makes anything or not. His labor demands the highest rate of pay and then loafs at every opportunity. As Mason puts it, "Every man in the district has his hand in Kingsley's pocket."

I don't like it. It's against my nature to see money wasted on service that isn't rendered and investments that aren't worth the price. And I don't think any of them are going to get rich quick. It is the decree from Above that we shall work for our living, and in one way or another, I think most everyone will. If anyone does get his money without working for it, I think he will be the unhappiest man of the lot.

September 2, 1947   Labor Day was celebrated yesterday in our town with the annual homecoming. All the prosperous folks, and the nice homey folks, who left many years ago for larger places, come back on homecoming day. They gather from the Pittsburgh district and Ohio and get to visit with one another as well as with old acquaintances here. Their acquaintances here are invariably the old folks. The young ones have grown up since they have gone. Our home-comers walk the streets where they used to race when they were children, sigh over rundown old buildings and talk of how pretty our town once was and could be made again if there was just the initiative and capital.

At noon the home-comers gather with the townsfolk under the oaks in the town square in front of the schoolhouse and eat picnic dinners. Yesterday was sunny, and the American Legion acted as host. They put benches and tables under the oaks and broadcasted music from a truck. They got the preachers to make a couple of prayers and corralled anyone they could find for speakers. After supper some fiddlers and a figure-caller got in the truck, and the young folks danced on the part of the square the school uses for a playground. The rest of us sat in chairs from the school auditorium and watched the dancers under a sunset sky till the dusk hid the twirling figures. Then we were told to take our chairs back to the auditorium for a free motion picture.

Halfway through the picture, someone told the packed auditorium there was a fire. There were no screams. The bewildered crowd just rose in the dark and moved toward the door with irresistible force. An old lady was pushed down, but someone helped her up. When we got out on the pavement, we learned Bill Brook's home about a mile out of town was burning down. We could see the light against the sky.

The men piled into cars and hurried to the scene while we women stood on the sidewalk talking quietly, sorry both for Brook's wife and that the holiday should have such an ending. Mary Brooks was the mother of five children and expecting another. Her home was a modern one, but her husband had been having financial reverses. Now she would lose everything. Folks said she was down at her sister's on Commercial Street, that no one was home when the fire started. Our town has no fire department, and there was not enough water at the Brook's to fight a fire. After a while I went down to the home where Mary was waiting.

She was sitting in the dark on the wide, vine-covered porch, crying softly. Her children, her sisters, and a neighbor or two sat with her. Other neighbors with extra beds came to offer them for the family. Having no extra one to offer, I could only express my sympathy.

September 10, 1947

The people have spoken, and the answer is "yes." Yes, they do want liquor and beer sold in our little town. From my station windows I could look down on the polls all day yesterday, watching the folks file in and out. The voters were orderly, and there was a watcher for each side. It was after dark when the election board gave out the totals and the wets learned they had won. Folks say they had a big celebration at the hotel last night.

But the effort was well worthwhile. Throughout the state the liquor interests and the officers of the law have learned the temper of the people and that they do want stricter enforcement of liquor regulations. They had to promise that to win a wet victory. Here the hotel keeper promises there will be no more liquor sold to drunks and no more brawls allowed. He is looking for a male bartender to replace his illegal female one. The vote here was 53 against the sale of either beer or liquor in the borough and 80 for it. Thirty-three voted for the candidates to be nominated but did not vote either way on the liquor argument. They did not want the liquor, but they thought it preferable to moon shining. Many others who stayed away from the polls entirely felt the same way. If some sensible, progressive plan toward temperance had been set before them, they would have voted for it.

September 20, 1947

The Ladies Bible Class met in the home of Lois Locke, who lives in the upstairs rooms of John Snyder's house, last night. That leader of the Democrat party here is a well-read bachelor, a sportsman, and has enough property to keep him without having to do any serious amount of work, but people shake their head over the way he has treated his house. It is too big for him, and he has refused to keep it in repair. He just re-roofed the part he wanted to live in. He lives in the downstairs rooms and has rented the upstairs to Lois and her husband. The rest of the house is slowly falling to pieces. All of the siding is off an upstairs room, leaving the interior exposed with some of its old furnishings as though someone had sliced off the outside wall. For a long time, a picture window hung precariously, but I think a March wind took care of it.

However, Lois's part of the upstairs is good solid oak floors and woodwork, and she has furnished it prettily. There was the usual business meeting last night, the usual chatting and laughter and refreshments, but the real purpose of the meeting was to give Mary Brooks a kitchen shower. Mary is staying with her sister till her husband can find a house for her, collect his insurance, and set them up at housekeeping again. Last night the women brought her everything in the way of a kitchen utensil they thought she would need. The Mill Run folks had previously given her a shower of other necessities. Also, the school children had taken up a donation for their schoolmates who had been burned out, and the women had taken Mary all their children's outgrown clothing that could be used, and made her emergency bed sheets out of cotton sacking.

Our hotheaded, warm-hearted little town.

September 27, 1947

The town seems to have settled down. There hasn't been a controversy all month. The school is humming orderly with two young ladies teaching the high school under principle Kozar, behaving as teachers should. One is new. One returned from last year. The directors, including Harry, are all soberly considering the school's financial plight. They have raised the school tax mileage, but that extra money will be needed to pay the teachers. It looks as though the students will strain their eyes in poor light and shiver in cold rooms for another term.

Squire Woodward is doing better at settling up his own affairs. He has sold his farm machinery and now only owns a barn and some pasture for cattle next summer. He says he has to keep something to make a living with. He liked the new idea of spraying paint on old buildings and has had his old store building near the station sprayed. A man who deals in secondhand furniture rents the storeroom for $10 a month and an old fellow batches in the upstairs for five. The Squire made a deal to pay $200 to have two coats of white paint sprayed on the place. His wife was astounded at him spending so much money on it.

"Why, Frank," she told him, "that old store building will last as long as we do!"

The Squire told her it would be good for somebody.

He dug his potatoes this week and cleaned off the garden. He is getting ready to loaf by the radiator in his office this winter, reading the papers, and sometimes the Bible, and listening to the radio. At prayer meeting Thursday evening, when Isabel asked for scripture verses, he arose and repeated his favorite:

"I have been young, and now am old; yet have I not seen the righteous forsaken, nor his seed begging bread."

The End.

More books by Shore Publications available at: ohiopyle.info, uniontownspeedway.com, Amazon, etc.

Ohiopyle, That Little Town WWII. McCahan $14.95
Speedway Kings, 100 Yrs of Racing History $34.95
Yesteryear at the Uniontown Speedway $24.95
1916 Uniontown Speedway Program reprint $10.00
Native Woody Landscape/Restoration Plants $30.00
Message of the Sacred Buffalo $15.00
Big Laurel Rising, Appalachian River Tale $12.00
Murder in Ohiopyle & Other Incidents $10.00
Gone to Ohiopyle (Illustrated History) $10.00
Hauntings of Pittsburgh & the Laurel Highlands $20.00
Butch's Smack Your Lips BBQ Cookbook $23.50
Yesteryear in Ohiopyle, Volume I $20.00
Yesteryear in Ohiopyle, Volume II $20.00
Yesteryear in Ohiopyle, Volume III $23.50
Yesteryear in Masontown $20.00
Yesteryear in Smithfield and Pt. Marion $20.00
Explorer's Guide to the Yough River/ Ohiopyle $15.00
Stone House Legends & Lore $12.00

Coming December 2012, *Murder in St. Michaels*
Coming Spring 2013, *Murder at the Vineyard & Other Mountain Tales*

Autographed copies available by mail order from Shore Publications, P. O. Box 111, Chalk Hill, PA 15421. FREE SHIPPING when you mention this book. Others, please send $5. to cover shipping costs.

Call McGuinnes to speak at your event: 724-710-2919.